FAMILY VIOLENCE

Volume 84, Sage Library of Social Research

Sage Library of Social Research

1 Caplovitz The Merchants of Harlem
2 Rosenau International Studies & the Social Sciences
3 Ashford Ideology & Participation
4 McGowan/Shapiro The Comparative Study of Foreign Policy
5 Male The Struggle for Power
6 Tanter Modelling & Managing International Conflicts
7 Catanese Planners & Local Politics
8 Prescott Economic Aspects of Public Housing
9 Parkinson Latin America, the Cold War, & the World Powers, 1945-1973
10 Smith Ad Hoc Governments
11 Gallimore et al Culture, Behavior & Education
12 Hallman Neighborhood Government in a Metropolitan Setting
13 Gelles The Violent Home
14 Weaver Conflict & Control in Health Care Administration
15 Schweigler National Consciousness in Divided Germany
16 Carey Sociology & Public Affairs
17 Lehman Coordinating Health Care
18 Bell/Price The First Term
19 Alderfer/Brown Learning from Changing
20 Wells/Marwell Self-Esteem
21 Robins Political Institutionalization & the Integration of Elites
22 Schonfeld Obedience & Revolt
23 McCready/Greeley The Ultimate Values of the
24 Nye Role Structure & Analysis of the Family
25 Wehr/Washburn Peace & World Order Systems
26 Stewart Children in Distress
27 Dedring Recent Advances in Peace & Conflict Research
28 Czudnowski Comparing Political Behavior
29 Douglas Investigative Social Research
30 Stohl War & Domestic Political Violence

31 Williamson Sons or Daughters
32 Levi Law & Politics in the International Society
33 Altheide Creating Reality
34 Lerner The Politics of Decision-Making
35 Converse The Dynamics of Party Support
36 Newman/Price Jails & Drug Treatment
37 Abercrombie The Military Chaplain
38 Gottdiener Planned Sprawl
39 Lineberry Equality & Urban Policy
40 Morgan Deterrence
41 Lefebvre The Structure of Awareness
42 Fontana The Last Frontier
43 Kemper Migration & Adaptation
44 Caplovitz/Sherrow The Religious Drop-Outs
45 Nagel/Neef The Legal Process: Modeling the System
46 Bucher/Stelling Becoming Professional
47 Hiniker Revolutionary Ideology & Chinese Reality
48 Herman Jewish Identity
49 Marsh Protest & Political Consciousness
50 LaRossa Conflict & Power in Marriage
51 Abrahamsson Bureaucracy or Participation
52 Parkinson The Philosophy of International Relations
53 Lerup Building the Unfinished
54 Smith Churchill's German Army
55 Corden Planned Cities
56 Hallman Small & Large Together
57 Inciardi et al Historical Approaches to Crime
58 Levitan/Alderman Warriors at Work
59 Zurcher The Mutable Self
60 Teune/Mlinar The Developmental Logic of Social Systems
61 Garson Group Theories of Politics
62 Medcalf Law & Identity
63 Danziger Making Budgets
64 Damrell Search for Identity

65 Stotland et al Empathy, Fantasy & Helping
66 Aronson Money & Power
67 Wice Criminal Lawyers
68 Hoole Evaluation Research & Development Activities
69 Singelmann From Agriculture to Services
70 Seward The American Family
71 McCleary Dangerous Men
72 Nagel/Neef Policy Analysis: In Social Science Research
73 Rejai/Phillips Leaders of Revolution
74 Inbar Routine Decision-Making
75 Galaskiewicz Exchange Networks & Community Politics
76 Alkin/Daillak/White Using Evaluations
77 Sensat Habermas & Marxism
78 Matthews The Social World of Old Women
79 Swanson/Cohen/Swanson Small Towns & Small Towners
80 Latour/Woolgar Laboratory Life
81 Krieger Hip Capitalism
82 Megargee/Bohn Classifying Criminal Offenders
83 Cook Who Should Be Helped?
84 Gelles Family Violence
85 Katzner Choice & the Quality of Life
86 Caplovitz Making Ends Meet
87 Berk/Berk Labor and Leisure at Home
88 Darling Families Against Society
89 Altheide/Snow Media Logic
90 Roosens Mental Patients in Town Life
91 Savage Founders, Heirs, & Managers
92 Bromley/Shupe "Moonies" in America
93 Littrell Bureaucratic Justice
94 Murray/Cox Beyond Probation
95 Roberts Afro-Arab Fraternity
96 Rutman Planning Useful Evaluations
97 Shimanoff Communication Rules
98 Laguerre Voodo Heritage
99 Macarov Work and Welfare

FAMILY VIOLENCE

Richard J. Gelles

Volume 84
SAGE LIBRARY OF
SOCIAL RESEARCH

 SAGE PUBLICATIONS   Beverly Hills   London

For information address:

SAGE PUBLICATIONS, INC.
275 South Beverly Drive
Beverly Hills, California 90212

SAGE PUBLICATIONS LTD
28 Banner Street
London EC1Y 8QE

Printed in the United States of America

Library of Congress Cataloging in Publication Data

Gelles, Richard J
   Family violence.

   (Sage library of social research; v. 84)
   Bibliography: p.
   1. Family violence—United States. I. Title.
HQ809.3.U5G44   301.42'7   79-14813
ISBN 0-8039-1234-X
ISBN 0-8039-1235-8 pbk.

38, 616

SECOND PRINTING

CONTENTS

Acknowledgements   9
Introduction   11

Part I: Violence Toward Children

Introduction   23
1 Child Abuse as Psychopathology:
  A Sociological Critique and Reformulation   27
2 The Social Construction of Child Abuse   43
3 Community Agencies and Child Abuse:
  Labeling and Gatekeeping   55
4 Violence Toward Children in the United States   73

Part II: Marital Violence

Introduction   91
5 Abused Wives: Why Do They Stay?   95
6 Violence and Pregnancy:
  A Note on the Extent of the Problem and Needed Services
7 Power, Sex, and Violence: The Case of Marital Rape   121
8 The Truth About Husband Abuse   137

Part III: Studying Family Violence

Introduction   145
9 Methods for Studying Sensitive Family Topics   147
10 Etiology of Violence: Overcoming Fallacious Reasoning in
   Understanding Family Violence and Child Abuse   169

Part IV: The Impact of Family Violence

Introduction   179
11 Family Experience and Public Support for the Death Penalty
   (with Murray A. Straus)   181

Cases   205
References   207
About the Author   219

To My Second Family, Max and Ann Isacoff

LIST OF TABLES AND FIGURES

Tables   *Page*

Psychopathological Model of Child Abuse   29
Types of Parent-to-Child Violence   81
Parent-to-Child Violence by Sex of Parent   84
Parent-to-Child Violence by Sex of Child   86
Parent-to-Child Violence in Past Year by Age of Child   87
Violence Severity by Intervention Mode   100
Intervention Mode by Wife's Experience with
Violence as a Child   102
Education, Occupation, Number of Children,
Age of Oldest Child by Intervention Mode   104
Step-wise Regression of Independent Variables and
Intervention and Intervention Modalities   106
Education by Child Abuse   176

Figures

A Social Psychological Model of the Causes of Child Abuse   38
A Model of the Process Producing Support for the
Death Penalty   199

ACKNOWLEDGEMENTS

I have been fortunate for the past eight years to have been able to draw on the help, guidance, and advice of many colleagues, friends, and students. I would not have been a student of family violence had it not been for Murray A. Straus. Murray has been a teacher, mentor, advisor, and morale booster during our partnership in the study of family violence. Each essay in this volume, each idea, each insight has much of Murray Straus's wisdom in it.

My study of family violence began at the University of New Hampshire. My colleagues and friends Howard Shapiro and Arnold Linsky provided significant guidance and support in the early years of my research.

My colleagues, students, and assistants at the University of Rhode Island have helped me, tolerated me, and counseled me since 1973. Michael Bassis, Terry Gebhart, Lucille Browning Cameron, Richard Pollnac, Martha Mulligan, Lana B. Israel, Joan Seites, and Eileen Hargreaves are all due a heartfelt thanks.

I have been fortunate to meet and have the help of many other colleagues in writing the articles included in this book. Eli Newberger, Cecilia Sudia, David Gil, Robert Lewis, Kathy DeHaven, Howard Erlanger, Marjorie Fields, and David Reiss all read and provided critical comments on at least one essay in this book.

Betty Jones, Beth Underwood, Lisa Belmont, and Sheryl Horwitz all tolerated my spelling and saw theirs ruined while typing manuscripts and essays included in this book. I apologize and appreciate their help.

Funding for the research reported in this book came from NIMH grants MH 15521, MH 13050, MH 24002, and MH 27557.

Funding also was provided by the National Center on Child Abuse and Neglect (Administration on Children, Youth and Families) #90-C-425.

I am grateful to Rhoda Blecker, Sara Miller McCune, and the staff of Sage Publications (past and present) for giving me an opportunity to bring these materials together into a book. I will always be in their debt for publishing my first book, THE VIOLENT HOME.

I owe my final and most important acknowledgement to my wife Judy, who made my research and writing tolerable and possible.

−R.J.G.

INTRODUCTION

People are more likely to be hit, beat up, physically injured, or even killed in their own homes by another family member than anywhere else, and by anyone else, in our society. Nearly one out of every four murder victims in the United States is killed by a member of one's own family, and this is the case in Africa, Great Britain, and Denmark (Straus et al., 1976; Bohannan, 1960; Curtis, 1974).

Each year in the United States, at least six million men, women, and children are victims of severe physical attacks at the hands of their spouses or parents—that is twice the population of the city of Los Angeles (Straus, Gelles, and Steinmetz, 1979). Imagine the entire student body of a large high school—2,000 students—suddenly killed by some catastrophic event. Each year 2,000 children are killed by their caretakers (this figure is cited in materials published by the National Center on Child Abuse and Neglect).

These facts are not new. We regularly hear about individual instances of family violence, and the history of child rearing and family relations are full of descriptions and discussions of child abuse and infanticide (Bakan, 1971; DeMause, 1974, 1975; Newberger, et. al., 1977; Radbill, 1974; Shorter, 1975). Yet, it has only been recently that these long-known facts about family violence have been pulled together into a general analysis of violence in the home. What formerly was thought of as individual aberrations or pathologies, is now seen as a pattern of family relations in millions of American families.

The criminal homicide statistics indicate that violence in the family is not strictly a social problem in the United States. Child beating and wife beating constitute significant social problems in Great Britain, Germany, Holland, and Israel. Beatrice Whiting, an anthropologist from Harvard University, noted that in her ethnographic research in Africa, as soon as people moved out of communal residences and established conjugal family residences, family members began to hit one another (1975). Her exact words were: "when the walls went up, people began to hit each other."

The study of violence in the home has typically focused on three major questions. First, there has been considerable concern over exactly how widespread the problem actually is. The concern with measuring the incidence of family violence is perhaps best explained as a reaction to the conventional wisdom that family violence is rare, recent, and confined to a few mentally disturbed people (Steinmetz and Straus, 1974). The second issue concerns patterns of family violence. Here the issues revolve around two contradictory points of view. On the one hand, some researchers argue that violence cannot be explained by social factors (see for example, Steele and Pollock, 1968; 1974). On the other hand, there is the "class myth" (Steinmetz and Straus, 1974; Pelton, 1978) which says that violence is confined to one social group (e.g., poor, Blacks, and the like). The third major question concerns what causes people to be violent. Early investigations of child abuse and wife beating employed a psychodynamic model of abuse and violence. These investigations were aimed at identifying personality traits and character disorders which were associated with, and caused people to physically attack family members. Other investigators developed sociological, social psychological, ecological, and various multidimensional theories of violence and abuse (for reviews of theories of violence see Gelles and Straus, 1979; Justice and Justice, 1976).

While the search for psychological disorders dominated the investigations of child abuse and family violence in the 1960s, the dominant model of the 1970s appears to be a social psychological approach. Skolnick and Skolnick (1977) sum up the present state of knowledge about the causes of family violence by stating that "Family violence seems to be a product of psychological tensions and external stresses affecting all families at all social levels." Empirical investigations of family violence support this claim and demonstrate that increased stress does increase the risk of abusive behavior in families (Newberger et. al., 1977; Straus et al., 1979).

Clearly, most of the empirical and theoretical work on family violence has focused at either the psychological or microsocial level of analysis. While this paradigm is fruitful and helpful in identifying areas where ameliorative efforts can be planned to treat and prevent family violence, such an approach tends to overlook the structural properties of the family and society which make the family violence-prone. The fact that family violence is typically not conceived of as a macrosocial issue is critically important, especially in light of Straus's argument that "at least 90 percent of the violence which takes place in American families grows out of the very nature of the family and the larger society, rather than out of individual aberrations" (1979a).

Violence and the Social Organization of the Family

In earlier work (Gelles and Straus, 1979) we tried to identify the unique characteristics of the family as a social group which contributed to making the family a violent-prone interaction setting. Later, Straus and Hotaling (1979), in reviewing these characteristics, noted the irony of the fact that these properties serve dual roles. On the one hand, they have the potential for making the family a warm, supportive, and intimate environment, on the other hand, they contribute to an organization which enhances the likelihood that violence will break out and escalate unchecked. Briefly, there were eleven factors:

(1) *Time at Risk.* The ratio of time spent interacting with family members far exceeds the ratio of time spent interacting with others, although the ratio will vary depending on stages in the family life cycle.

(2) *Range of Activities and Interests.* Not only do family members spend a great deal of time with one another, the interaction ranges over a much wider spectrum of activities than nonfamilial interaction.

(3) *Intensity of Involvement.* The quality of family interaction is also unique. The degree of commitment to family interaction is greater. A cutting remark made by a family member is likely to have a much larger impact than the same remark in another setting.

(4) *Impinging Activities.* Many interactions in the family are inherently conflict-structured and have a "zero sum" aspect. Whether it involves deciding what television show to watch or what car to buy, there will be both winners and losers in family relations.

(5) *Right to Influence.* Belonging to a family carries with it the implicit right to influence the values, attitudes, and behaviors of other family members.

(6) *Age and Sex Differences.* The family is unique in that it is made up of different ages and sexes. Thus, there is the potential for a battle between generations *and* sexes.

(7) *Ascribed Roles.* In addition to the problem of age and sex differences is the fact that the family is perhaps the only social institution which assigns roles and responsibilities based on age and sex rather than interest or competence.

(8) *Privacy.* The modern family is a private institution, insulated from the eyes, ears, and often rules of the wider society. Where privacy is high, the degree of social control will be low (Laslett, 1973).

(9) *Involuntary Membership.* Families are exclusive organizations. Birth relationships are involuntary and cannot be terminated. While there can be ex-wives and ex-husbands, there are no ex-children or ex-parents (Rossi, 1968). Being in a family involves personal, social, material, and legal commitment and entrapment. When conflict arises it is not easy to break off the conflict by fleeing the scene or resigning from the group.

(10) *Stress.* Families are prone to stress. This is due in part to the theoretical notion that dyadic relationships are unstable (Simmel, 1950). Moreover, families are constantly undergoing changes and transitions. The birth of children, maturation of children, aging, retirement, and death are all changes which are recognized by family scholars (LeMasters, 1957). Moreover, stress felt by one family member (such as unemployment, illness, bad grades at school) is transmitted to other family members.

(11) *Extensive Knowledge of Social Biographies.* The intimacy and emotional involvement of family relations reveals a full range of identities to members of a family. Strengths and vulnerabilities, likes and dislikes, loves and fears are all known to family members. While this knowledge can help support a relationship, the information can also be used to attack intimates and lead to conflict (Goode, 1971).

Cultural Norms and Family Violence

It is one thing to say that the social organization of the family makes the family a conflict-prone institution and social group.

However, the 11 characteristics which we listed do not supply necessary or sufficient conditions for violence. The fact that the social organization of the family which we have just described exists within a cultural context where violence is tolerated, accepted, and even mandated provides the key link between family organization and violent behavior. Opinion and attitude surveys find a high level of support for violence outside and within the home (Stark and McEvoy, 1970). In a nationally representative sample of adults 70% feel it is good for boys to get in a few fist fights while growing up (Stark and McEvoy, 1970). One in four Americans feel it is acceptable for a husband to hit his wife under certain conditions (Stark and McEvoy, 1970).

The widespread acceptability and use of physical punishment to raise children creates a situation where a conflict-prone institution serves as a training ground to teach children that it is acceptable: (1) to hit people you love, (2) for powerful people to hit less powerful people, (3) to use hitting to achieve some end or goal, and (4) to hit as an end in itself.

An Exchange Model of Family Violence

To put it simply, people hit family members because they can. Although people may learn that hitting and violence can be an appropriate or accepted response when experiencing frustration or stress, there are a number of factors which constrain people from being violent when they encounter stress and frustration. First, there is the potential of being hit back. Second, a violent assault could lead to arrest and/or imprisonment. Finally, using violence could lead to a loss of status. Thus, typically, there are costs involved in being violent (Goode, 1971).

The social organization of the family serves to reduce the potential costs of a person being violent towards a spouse or children.

Inequality. The normative power structure in the society and the family and the resulting sexual and generational inequality in the family serves to reduce the chances that victims of family violence can threaten or inflict harm on offenders. Husbands are typically bigger than wives, have higher status positions, and earn more money. Because of this, they can use violence without worrying about being struck hard enough to be injured or having their wives take economic or social sanctions against them. Parents can use violence on children without fear that their children can strike back and injure them. By and large, women and child victims of family violence have no place to run and are not strong enough or possess enough resources to inflict costs on their attackers.

Privacy. Victims of family violence could turn to outside agencies to redress their grievances, but the private nature of the family reduces the accessibility of outside agencies of social control. Neighbors who report that they overhear incidents of family violence also say that they fear intervening in another person's home. Police, prosecutors, and courts are reluctant to pursue cases involving domestic violence. When these cases are followed up the courts are faced with the no-win position of either doing nothing or separating the combatants. Thus, to protect a child, judges may view as their only alternative to remove the child from the home. To protect the woman, the solution may be a separation or divorce. Either situation puts the legal system in the position of breaking up a family to protect individual members. Because courts typically view this as a drastic step, such court-ordered separations or removals are comparatively rare, unless there is stark evidence of repeated grievous injury.

Violence and the "real man." One last cost of being violent is the loss of social status that goes along with being labeled a "child beater" or a "wife beater." However, there are subcultural groups where aggressive sexual and violent behavior is considered proof that someone is a real man. Thus, rather than risk status loss, the violent family member may actually realize a status gain.

In situations where status can be lost by being violent, individuals employ accepted vocabularies of motive (Mills, 1940) or "accounts" (Lyman and Scott, 1970) to explain their untoward behavior. Thus, a violent father or mother might explain their actions by saying they were drunk or lost control. Parents who shared the same desire to batter their children might nod in agreement without realizing that a real loss of control would have produced a much more grievous injury or even death.

Primary and Secondary Prevention of Family Violence

We said earlier that the study of family violence has focused on three major questions—incidence, social and psychological factors associated with violence, and the causes of family violence. Implicit in each of these empirical issues is the search for knowledge which can be used to prevent and treat violence in the home.

Researchers and practitioners have been careful to point out that there are two types of "solutions" to the problem of family violence—intervention and treatment after an incident of violence occurs and prevention of violence before it takes place (see for example, Justice and Justice, 1976).

There have been numerous suggestions and implementations of programs aimed at treating known cases of family violence and preventing further abusive behavior. Psychological and family counseling programs, behavior modification, self-help groups—such as Parents Anonymous, shelters, crisis nurseries and day care centers, comprehensive emergency social services, and many other programs have been developed to assist families which have been publicly identified as abusive. As we state in the first essay in this book, such programs are useful and necessary, but they serve only as ambulances at the bottom of the cliff. Given that the incidence of family violence runs to the millions of families, there are not nearly enough resources or programs to meet the needs of all violent families. A related point is that because there are insufficient resources and because child and wife beating are stigmatized behavior, only a fraction of violent families will either come to public attention or admit that they need help. The more cynical observers of current theory and practice in the field of violence in the home bemoan the fact that present treatment programs are nothing more than band-aids for bleeding arteries. While there is a grain of truth in this argument, it drastically oversimplifies the issue. If, as we argue, the widespread incidence and severity of family violence is a product of cultural norms which tolerate and approve of violence and the particular social organization of the family, then the ultimate solution and the most effective programs of primary prevention will have to recognize that no meaningful change can occur until something is done to change prevailing cultural norms and alter the social organization of the family.

To prevent violence, we need to take steps to eliminate the norms and values which legitimize and glorify violence in the society and the family. A society which creates and supports norms and values that legitimize and glorify violence will be a society that has a high level of family violence (Straus, 1977a). Nearly half of all American homes have guns in them (Stark and McEvoy, 1970). Television, movies, and even children's literature (Huggins and Straus, 1979) glorify heroes who solve problems and express themselves through acts of physical aggression. Our government legitimizes violence by supporting capital punishment for severe crimes and even supporting corporal punishment in schools. We require (and are beginning to see) public awareness campaigns which outline and detail the extent and seriousness of violence in the family. America requires domestic disarmament (Straus, 1977a). Gun control is necessary, not to keep guns out of the hands of criminals, but to protect family members—the most frequent victims of murders involving firearms! To reduce violence in the home we must reduce violence in society. The death penalty should be eliminated, and corporal punishment in schools banned. Violence on television should also be reduced. In short, the hitting license in America must be cancelled (Straus, 1977a). If family violence is to be reduced, we need values and norms which say: People are not for hitting.

A second step towards reducing violence is to reduce the stress which limits individuals' and families' abilities to cope with conflict in their homes. Violence in the home can possibly be reduced if we have full employment, an elimination of poverty, guaranteed health care for all individuals, and abortion on demand. The average person reading this passage will say, "but that is expensive" or "that is impossible." Granted it is expensive, granted it may seem impossible. The issue is that we have grown to accept a society which has poverty, which has unemployment, and which blocks access to health care and social positions. But, society does not have to be organized in this manner, and it will have to change if we are to realize any decline in the level of family violence.

Next, the sexist character of society must change. An underlying cause of family violence is the fact that the family is perhaps the only social group where jobs, tasks and responsibilities are assigned on the basis of gender and age, rather than interest or ability (Gelles, 1974). An elimination of the concept of "women's work"; elimination of the taken-for-granted view that the husband is and must be the head of the family; and an elimination of sex-typed family roles are all prerequisites to the reduction of family violence (Straus, 1977a).

Fourth, we must break the cycle of violence breeding violence in the family. We must reduce and gradually eliminate the use of physical punishment of children and develop alternative parenting techniques which do not depend on hitting or force. Children should not learn that it is acceptable to hit those whom they love.

Finally, we must accelerate changes in legal codes and court systems and move the courts away from the traditional view that family conflict is an area where the courts should not intervene. Women and children require, and are entitled to, equal legal protection under the law. Wives should be able to prosecute their husbands for assault or rape. The court procedures for dealing with domestic violence need to be streamlined. And last, police should be trained to cope with and manage domestic disputes.

These solutions are all based on information gathered through research on violence in the family. The solutions proposed all involve long-term and radical changes in the fabric of a society which now tends to tolerate, encourage, and accept the use of violence in families.

Many of these proposals challenge taken-for-granted ideas of individual and group rights. Some of the proposals imply a reduction of privacy in the home and an element of intervention by government into the daily affairs of families. Clearly, some of the proposals are controversial, some are costly, and some, given the way we are taught to think about life in America, seem unworkable. However, the alternative is the continuation of a deadly tradition of domestic violence. No meaningful change will take place without some social and familial change, and this will mean a change in the fundamental way we organize our lives, our families, and our society.

Scope of the Book

In the last decade there have been numerous books published on battered children or battered wives. There have been a few books which chose to conceptualize the problem as a family issue rather than a problem of children or women. Throughout our eight-year program of research we have viewed child battering and wife battering as pieces of a larger puzzle—violence in the family. Our empirical evidence confirms our early hypothesis that the various forms of family violence are related. This reaffirms our conviction that family violence is an issue of family relations rather than just a problem of child rearing or conflict between spouses. We find that children who grow up in violent homes go on to use violence on their own spouses and children. Our current research (Straus et al., 1979) finds that children who see their parents hit one another and children who are hit by their parents are more likely to use violence on their siblings and on their parents than children raised in nonviolent settings.

This book brings together 10 previously published essays (in revised and updated form) and one new essay on family violence. These essays are the product of three closely related research projects. The first project was an indepth series of interviews with 80 families which focused on the incidence, types, nature, and patterns of violence between husbands and wives (Gelles, 1974). Our first book on family violence, *The Violent Home* presented data on the extent of violence, the types of violence which are used, and the social factors which are related to marital violence. After the study and the book were completed, a number of important questions prompted us to continue to analyze our interview data. We were concerned with three questions: why did some of the women we interviewed who reported that they were beaten by their husbands choose to stay with their assaultive spouses? Over and over again we were asked why battered wives stayed at risk and did not call the police, run away, or try to get a divorce. A second issue, which we touched on briefly in the first book was that pregnant women were extremely vulnerable to being victims of domestic violence. Why was this the case, and what could be done about it? The third question arose while the first book was being copy-edited. One of the editors wrote us a short note which asked why we failed to consider sexual violence between husbands and wives. The idea of "marital rape" had never occurred to us at any time in the design, carrying out, analysis, and reporting of the research. But, the more we thought about the question, the more we realized that it was a significant issue in the study of marital violence. The three essays which address these questions are contained in Part II of this volume, "Marital Violence."

The first essay we ever wrote on family violence is the initial essay in this book. "Child Abuse as Psychopathology: A Sociological Critique and Reformulation" applied social psychological theory to the problem of child abuse. We found the research and theoretical conceptions of child abuse sorely lacking in sophistication and evidence. Our first essay on this subject led us to a second study of family violence. Nearly all the conferences we attended in the first five years of our research devoted major blocks of time to trying to define child abuse. After five years, it quickly became evident that there could never be an accepted or acceptable definition of child abuse. And yet, child abuse was being defined each day by social service workers and physicians who applied labels such as "child abuse" and "child maltreator" to suspicious injuries in children they encountered. We became curious about the process which led some children to be labeled as "abused" and some children to be classified as "accidentally injured"—even though their injuries were the same. Thus, we began a three-year investigation of the social construction of child abuse. Our theoretical essay, "The Social Construction of Child Abuse," and a previously unpublished work, "Community Agencies and Child Abuse: Labeling and Gatekeeping" are included in Part I of this volume "Violence Toward Children."

Ever since we began our first exploratory study of family violence we were regularly asked, "how extensive is family violence?" and "what causes people to be violent toward family members?" Yet, despite years of research, there were no studies which satisfied basic rules of evidence and could be used to estimate the national rates of family violence. Available research suffered from a number of flaws, some of which are discussed in "Etiology of Violence: Overcoming Fallacious Reasoning in Understanding Family Violence and Child Abuse," in Part III of this volume. With Murray Straus and Suzanne Steinmetz, we spent three years planning a national survey of violence in the American family. The long planning period was needed to assess and try to overcome some of the methodological problems we anticipated running into in such a large-scale research project. One of the first products of the study was an essay reviewing methods which could be used to study sensitive family topics ("Methods for Studying Sensitive Family Topics," in Part III of this volume). Our national survey of 2,143 families allowed us to estimate the extent of violence towards children and violence between husbands and wives. We found rates of family violence which were considerably greater than we had anticipated. Not only that, we also encountered some unusual data. Our study found that more husbands were victims of severe violence than wives. Does this mean that husband abuse is more common than wife abuse and is a greater social problem? We think not. Our essay, "The Truth About Husband Abuse" tries to go beyond the raw data generated by our national study and get at the real meaning of what constitutes "abuse." This essay also briefly summarizes some of the social factors we found related to family violence in the United States.

The book concludes with a theoretical essay which links violence in the home to support for violence outside the family. In "Family Experience and Public Support for the Death Penalty" we confront the disturbing evidence that the effects of family violence are not confined within the home.

PART I

VIOLENCE TOWARD CHILDREN

Introduction

VIOLENCE TOWARD CHILDREN

During the last 10 years increasing public attention directed at the problem of abused and neglected children has made it seem like child abuse is a new phenomenon, or if it is not new, it is probably becoming more widespread. Historical evidence suggests that child abuse and violence toward children go back to colonial times in America and to Biblical times in the history of man (Bakan, 1971; DeMause, 1974, 1975; Newberger et. al., 1977; Radbill, 1974). Recent attention to child abuse as a social problem has been described as a product of radiologists seeking the potential for increased prestige, role expansion, and coalition formation with psychiatry and pediatrics (Pfohl, 1977).

One thing is clear, beginning with the application of X-ray technology to the "discovery" of child abuse cases (Caffey, 1946), through Kempe et al.'s groundbreaking essay on the "battered baby syndrome" in the Journal of the American Medical Association (1962), continuing with the passage of legislation requiring the reporting of child abuse and neglect cases in all 50 states in the late 1960s, and culminating in the passage by Congress of the Child Abuse and Prevention Act and establishment of the National Center on Child Abuse and Neglect in 1974, there has been a persistent and increased attention focused on the problem of the abuse and neglect of children.

The major issues in the study of child abuse and neglect have been (1) the need to develop an adequate definition of child abuse and neglect, (2) the desire to accurately measure how extensive the problem of abuse and neglect is in the United States (and other countries), (3) a search for the causes of child maltreatment, and (4) the desire to "do something" about child abuse and develop significant modes of primary and secondary prevention.

The first problem has yet to be solved, and there is some question as to whether it can ever be resolved. There presently is no useful legal or scientific definition of child abuse and neglect. This is perhaps because child abuse is a political concept rather than a legal or scientific one. While the definition of abuse may read: "any act by a parent or caretaker which intentionally injures a child—either physically or mentally"; establishing intent and determining what constitutes an injury is a major dilemma. As Newberger and Bourne (1978) state, a main problem in identifying cases of child abuse is the tendency to label intentionally caused injuries as accidents (there also is the problem of labeling accidents abusive injuries).

In our own program of research we have chosen to study child abuse and neglect by selecting a specific, measurable phenomenon—violence towards children. In doing this we have the advantage of being able to focus on a specific concept without having to worry about problems of intent and injury. For our purposes in conducting the study which led to the essay, "Violence Toward Children in the United States" we focused only on seven acts of violence.

A second problem in the study of child abuse and neglect has been to determine which individuals and families are the most likely to abuse their children and then use these data to build a causal explanation of child abuse. In the first essay in this section, "Child Abuse as Psychopathology: A Sociological Critique and Reformulation" we constructed a model of the causes of child abuse from the available data which had been published by physicians, social workers, and psychiatrists. The data supported our contention that child abuse, rather than being a product of some mental aberration or psychological problem with the caretaker, grows out of a complex set of interrelated social, psychological, environmental, and ecological factors.

Only after we published the "Social Psychological Model of Child Abuse" did we realize that it was based on a weak foundation. The model was based on data from affirmed cases which had been publicly labeled child abuse. The process of labeling determines what our estimate of the incidence of abuse will be, provides the data for our causal models and empirical generalizations about child abuse, and ultimately suggests what the appropriate intervention, treatment, and prevention programs should be. But all these pieces of information are based on only a fraction of the total number of actual abuse cases. In the course of our research we asked, "Are low-income families more likely to abuse their children, or to get caught abusing their children?" It appears that the answer is "all of the above." Official reports of child abuse overrepresent low-income families and our own national survey of family violence (which was free from the bias of using reported cases and which used a representative sample of families in the United States) found that those with the lowest incomes are more likely to abuse their children (Gelles, 1978b; Straus, 1979b; Straus et al., 1979). Our national survey went on to find that stress, unemployment and underemployment, number of children, and social isolation were all related to abusive violence towards children.

The essays which follow emphasize two paths of investigating the problem of violence towards children and child abuse. The first, more traditional direction is a search for the answer to the questions of how extensive child abuse is and what causes people to abuse their children. From our national survey we conclude that there are no fewer than 1.5 million children each year who are physically abused by their parents. The roots of abuse appear to be located in a complex interrelationship of social and psychological factors. One thing of which we are convinced, mental illness and psychiatric disorder are not the sole causes of abusive behavior by parents and caretakers.

The second stream of thought represented in the following essays focuses on the agents and agencies who first come into contact with child abuse and neglect cases. How do these gatekeepers define child abuse? What kinds of people and families are labeled abusive? What kinds of families and people are missed by the labelers? We have pursued this issue because we recognize that even if we can properly define child abuse, measure its incidence, and determine its cause, we will not be able to do much about it without a knowledgeable and capable protective services system. To determine the state of the art in protective services we need to focus some of our research energy on how they operate as well as try to answer the fundamental questions about child abuse and its causes.

Chapter 1

CHILD ABUSE AS PSYCHOPATHOLOGY:

A SOCIOLOGICAL CRITIQUE AND REFORMULATION

Each year in this country, thousands of children are brutally beaten, abused, and sometimes killed by their mothers and fathers. The dominant theme of research on this problem has been the use of a "psychopathological model" of child abuse—the parent who abuses suffers from a psychological pathology or sickness that accounts for abusing or battering a child.

This essay takes a critical look at the psychopathological theory of child abuse and finds a number of deficiencies with the model. First, this explanation of child abuse is too narrow. It posits a single causal variable (a presumed mental aberration or disease) to account for child abuse, while it ignores other variables that this essay will show are equally or more important causal factors. Second, psychopathology theory is inconsistent in stating that abuse is caused by a pathology, while many of the research reports

Reprinted, with permission, from the American Journal of Orthopsychiatry. Copyright 1973 by the American Orthopsychiatric Association, Inc.

state that all abusers are not psychopaths. Finally, close examination of the literature on child abuse shows that it is not based on research that meets even the minimal standards of evidence in social science (Spinetta and Rigler, 1972).

The purpose of this essay is to provide a more dimensional analysis of the generative sources of child abuse. The analysis goes beyond the unicausal approach of the psychopathology model; it analyzes sociocultural features of the abuser such as socioeconomic status, sex, employment status, and previous experience with violence, and it relates these to such factors as the age, temperament, and sib-order of the abused child. In addition, the social context of child abuse is examined.

The essay concludes with a broader, social-psychological model of child abuse and discusses the implications of this approach for strategies of intervention in child abuse.

The Psychopathological Model[1]

THE CHILD ABUSER: A PSYCHOPATHIC PORTRAIT

Essays on child abuse almost invariably open by asserting that a parent who would inflict serious abuse on a child is in some manner sick. This assertion ranges from the point blank statement that the child abusing parent is mentally ill (Coles, 1964) to the indirect statement that the abuser is the patient of the clinician (Bennie and Sclare, 1969). In some cases, the sickness is traced to a flaw in the socialization process, where "something went haywire or was not touched in the humanization process" (Wasserman, 1967). Many essays and books begin with the assumption that the parent abuser is a psychopath. Steele and Pollock (1968) announce that their first parent abuser was a "gold mine of psychopathology"; Kempe et al. (1962) describe the abuser as the "psychopathological member of the family"; while Galdston (1965) mentions parents who "illustrate their psychopathology" when discussing their relations with their children.

The psychopathological model goes on to focus on specific psychological characteristics of the parent. Steele and Pollock (1968) hold that child abusing parents have severe emotional problems, while Kempe et al. (1962) locate the problem in a

defect of the character structure. The parent who abuses is described as impulsive, immature, and depressed (Steele and Pollock,
1968; Kempe et al., 1962; Bennie and Sclare, 1969; Zalba, 1971).
A link between sex and violence in the abusive parent is shown in
the findings that abusive parents are sadomasochistic (Steele and
Pollock, 1968) and that they abuse their children to displace
aggression and sadism (Bennie and Sclare, 1969). Abusive parents
are also described as having poor emotional control (Bennie and
Sclare, 1969) and quick to react with poorly controlled aggression
(Kempe et al., 1962). Some authors describe the child abuser as
inadequate (Bennie and Sclare, 1969), self-centered and hyper-
sensitive (Kempe et al., 1962), having pervasive anger (Zalba,
1971), and dependent, egocentric, narcissistic, demanding, and
insecure (Steele and Pollock, 1968). Abusive parents also suffer
from some psychosomatic illnesses (Steele and Pollock, 1968) and
have a perverse fascination with punishment of children (Young,
1964).

Many other authors (U.S. Department of Health, Education and
Welfare, 1969) could be cited as illustration that the psychopathological model views the abusing parent as having abnormal
psychological traits. However, those works cited are sufficient to
make clear that mental abnormality is viewed as the cause of child
abuse.

PARENT AND CHILD: REVEALING THE PSYCHOPATHY

The authors advancing the psychopathological model of child
abuse find the disorder manifested in the parent's relationship
with his child. One form of this manifestation is the "transference
psychosis" (Galdston, 1965). Abusive parents often speak of their
child as if he were an adult; they perceive the child as a hostile
persecuting adult, and often see former guilt in their own child
(Galdston, 1965). As a result of the "transference," the parental

Table 1: Psychopathological Model of Child Abuse

Early Childhood Experience ⟶	Psychopathic States ⟶	Child Abuse
Abused	Personality traits	
Emotionally abandoned	Character traits	
Psychologically abandoned	Poor control	
Physical punishment	Neurological states	

distortion of reality causes a misinterpretation of the infant child. The child is perceived as the psychotic portion of the parent, which the parent wishes to destroy (Steele and Pollock, 1968). The child is projected as the cause of the parent's troubles (Steele and Pollock, 1968) and becomes a "hostility sponge" for the parent (Wasserman, 1967).

The psychopathy of the abusive parent is conceived as manifesting itself as a transference and distortion of reality on the part of the parent. In this state, the immature, impulsive, dependent (and the like) individual lashes out at a hostile world. More specifically, he lashes out at what he projects as the source of his troubles—his child.

CAUSE OF THE PSYCHOPATHY

After identifying the abusive parent as sick, listing the traits or symptoms of the sickness, and illustrating how the sickness manifests itself in parent-child relations, the psychopathological model establishes a causal explanation for the presence of the psychopathy. Steele and Pollock (1968) state that one cause is that the parents were raised in the same style (physical punishment and abuse) they re-create in raising their own children. This position is elaborated by Reiner and Kaufman (1959), who find that abusive parents are imbedded depressives because they were emotionally or psychologically abandoned as a child; as a result, violent behavior becomes the child's means of communication. This establishes a life pattern of aggression and violence, which explains both the psychopathy and the abuse (Bennie and Sclare, 1969). Thus, the cause of the pathology is the parent's early childhood experience, which included abuse and abandonment. The assumption is that parents who were abused as children will almost certainly pass this on to their own children.

The resulting psychopathological model is diagrammed in Table 1; it is an elementary linear model. Early childhood experience characterized by abuse creates psychological stress that produces certain psychopathic states. These psychopathic conditions, in turn, cause abusive acts toward the child.

PROBLEMS OF THE PSYCHOPATHOLOGICAL MODEL

A problem of the psychopathological approach is that most of the discussions of the causes of child abuse are clearly inconsistent and contradictory. Some authors contradict themselves by first stating that the abusing parent is a psychopath and then stating that the child abuser is no different from the rest of society. Steele and Pollock (1968) state that their first patient was a "gold mine of psychopathology," and then later state that their patients were a "random cross-section of the general population" who "would not seem much different than a group of people picked by stopping the first several dozen people one would meet on a downtown street." Zalba (1971) states that child abusers do not fit easily into a psychiatric category, while Galdston (1965) maintains that, aside from the transference psychosis, there are no other symptoms of psychotic disorder. Kempe et al. (1962) after describing the psychopathic personality of the child abuser, goes on to state that child beating is not confined to people with psychopathic disorders.

A second problem is an inability to pinpoint the personality traits that characterize the pathology. Of 19 traits listed by the authors, there was agreement by two or more authors on only four traits. Each remaining trait was mentioned by only a single author. Thus, there is little agreement as to the makeup of the psychopathy.

A third problem is that few studies attempt to test any hypothesis concerning the phenomenon. A recent comprehensive review of the literature (Spinetta and Rigler, 1972) found that most of the studies start and end with relatively untested common-sense assumptions. This, in turn, is because most of the studies are ex post facto (Spinetta and Rigler, 1972). When the analysis of the behavior takes place after the fact, little analytic understanding of the genesis of the behavior is offered. For instance, authors state that abusive parents have poor emotional control (Bennie and Sclare, 1969), or that they react with poorly controlled aggression (Kempe et al., 1962). Analyzed after the fact, it seems obvious that a parent who beats his child almost to the point of death has poor emotional control and reacts with uncontrolled aggression. This type of analysis does not distinguish the behavior in question from the explanation. The drawbacks of this type of labeling are pointed out by Szasz (1960, 1961, 1970) in his discussion of the myth of mental illness. Szasz argues that people who are labeled mentally ill are *then* thought to be suffering from mental illness. The types of after-the-fact explanations offered by the psychopathologic model offer little predictive power in the study of child abuse.

A final criticism of the psychopathological approach is the sampling technique used to gather the data. Most of the data are gathered from cases that medical or psychiatric practitioners have at hand. Thus, the sample cannot be considered truly representative of child abusers because many or most are not seen in clinics. More importantly, there is no attempt to compare samples of "patients" with any comparative group of nonchild abusers. Without this comparison, we have no way of knowing whether, in fact, child abusers differ from the rest of the population in terms of the causal variables proposed by the psychopathological model.[2]

A Sociological Approach to Child Abuse

It should be noted that authors advancing the psychopathological model make a special effort to point out that social variables *do not* enter into the causal scheme of child abuse. Steele and Pollock (1968), for instance, state that social, economic, and demographic factors are irrelevant to the actual act of child beating. Other researchers (Blumberg, 1964; Galdston, 1965; Young, 1964; Zalba, 1971) also argue that their cases of child abuse make up a cross-section of socioeconomic status, ethnicity, age, and education.

In examining the data presented in the research on child abuse it is apparent that, even though the authors deny the relevancy of social factors, there are patterns of sociological and contextual variables that *are* associated with child abuse.[3] This section reexamines the data in terms of three aspects of child abuse: the social characteristics of abusing parents, the social characteristics of the victims, and the situational or contextual properties of the act of child abuse. This section is aimed at broadening our understanding of the causes of child abuse by examining the sociological features of the abusers, abused, and acts of abuse.

THE PARENT WHO ABUSES

Even though the authors note that their case materials evidence a large number of middle-class parents, there is evidence that the working and lower classes are overrepresented among child abusers. The essays that provide data on the socioeconomic class of each abuser show an association between social class and child abuse. Gil (1971) found that, in most of his cases, the perpetrator of the abuse was of low socioeconomic status. Bennie and Sclare (1969) found that 80% of their cases of child abuse (10 cases) were from the lower class (unskilled workers). Factors related to socioeconomic status also support the notion of the low status of the abuser. Gil (1971) reports that education, occupation, and income of child abusers are lower than those of the general population. Galdston (1965) states that battering parents have limited education and financial means.

This evidence lends support to the claims that intrafamily violence occurs more often in the lower class or the working class. Blumberg (1964) points out that the lower class uses "normal violence" more often than do upper classes. Steinmetz and Straus (1971), while arguing that the literature is not conclusive,[4] do concede that intrafamily violence is more common among the working class. In explaining his findings, Gil (1971) argues that the socioeconomic pressures on the lower class weaken the caretakers' psychological mechanisms of self-control; he feels that the poverty of the lower classes produces frustration that is released in a physical attack on the child.

Another finding in the sociological analysis of child abuse is that the sex of the abuser is often female. Resnick's study of child filicide found that mothers kill more often than fathers (1969: 88-43). Of Bennie and Sclare's (1969) 10 cases of abuse, seven of the abusers were women. Steele and Pollock (1968) report that, of their 57 cases of child abuse, the mother was the abuser 50 times. In Zalba's (1971) study, the sexes split 50-50 in terms of who was the actual abusing parent. Gil's (1971) analysis of cases found that the mother abused children 50% of the time, while the father abused children 40%. (Gil also determined that the reason for this might be the predominance of female-headed households.)

Given the culturally defined male-aggressive/female-passive roles in our society and that men are usually more aggressive than women (Singer, 1971), it might be surprising that females are so highly represented and overrepresented in cases of child abuse. One explanation for this is that the child threatens or interferes with the mother's identify and esteem more than it does the father's. (Except when the father cannot fill the provider role, and children can be seen as a threat to his identity and esteem [O'Brien, 1971].) An illustration of this hypothesis is a case cited by Galdston (1965), in which a mother had to quit work as a result of a pregnancy and her husband's desire to return to work. Forced into closer contact with her 10-month-old child, she subsequently beat him because she found his cries "so demanding." Other case studies indicate that it is the mother who, through close contact with the child, experiences the frustration of trying to rear and control the child. The child who is perceived by the mother as impinging on her freedom and desires seems to be vulnerable to abuse from the frustrated mother.

THE CHILD WHO IS ABUSED

The most dangerous period for the child is from 3 months of age to 3 years. The abused, battered, or murdered child is most vulnerable during those years when he is most defenseless and least capable of meaningful social interaction. Resnick (1969) found that the first six months were the most dangerous for the child. Bennie and Sclare (1969) report that, in their sample, battered children were usually from 2 to 4 months old. Kempe et al., (1962) stated that the "Battered Child Syndrome" was most common in children under 3 years of age, while Galdston (1965) found that the most frequent cases of abuse were from 3 months to 3-and-a-half years. It is entirely possible that these data are somewhat misleading, because the vulnerability of a child to physical damage is greater the younger he is. Older children may also be subject to physical abuse, but they might not appear in medical case studies because their age-produced physical durability makes them less vulnerable to serious physical damage caused by abuse.

There are two analytic directions that can be followed. The first is that there is something about parental relations with young, subsocial children that leads some parents to abuse them; the second is that parental abuse of children is not a function of the child's age and that the data are misleading by nonrepresentative and selective gathering of cases. At this point, I would opt for the first direction. There seem to be three interrelated factors that result in the 3-month to 3-year-old child being particularly vulnerable to parental abuse.

First, the small infant or toddler lacks the physical durability to withstand much physical punishment or force. While an older child might absorb a great deal of physical punishment, the 3 month to 3 year old is likely to be severely damaged or even killed by the same type of force. Thus, because younger children are more likely to be harmed, they are more easily *abused*. Second, the fact that infants are not capable of much meaningful social interaction may create a great deal of frustration for parents who are trying to interact with infants. The case studies reveal that abusing parents often complain that they hit their children because they could not toilet-train them, get them to stop crying, or get them to obey their commands. Because the parents cannot "reason" with infants, they may feel their only course of action is physical punishment.

Third, the new or infant child may create stress for the parent just by birth alone. The new-born child may create economic hardship for the family, or may interfere with professional, occupational, educational, or other plans of the parents. Thus, the new child may create structural stress for parents which is responded to by abuse.

THE SOCIAL CONTEXT

Perhaps the best example of the narrowness of the psychopathological approach to child abuse is the fact that it does not examine possible social causes of the psychological stress that it sees as leading to child abuse.

One stress-producing condition is unemployment. O'Brien (1971) in his discussion of the causes of intrafamily violence, argues that one should find violence most common in families whose classically dominant member (male-adult-husband) fails to possess the superior skills, talents, or resources on which his preferred superior status is supposed to be based. O'Brien's theory would support the notion that unemployment of the husband would lead to intrafamily violence. This assumption is supported in the child abuse literature. Gil (1971) found that nearly half of the fathers of abused children were not employed at the time of the abusive act. Galdston (1965) also found that, in abusive families, the father of the abused child was unemployed or worked part time while the wife worked part time and cared for the child the rest of the time.

A second contextual factor is that the abused child is usually the product of an unwanted pregnancy. The Massachusetts Society for the Prevention of Cruelty to Children reports that in 50% of 115 families studied, there was premarital conception (Zalba, 1971). Wasserman (1967) found that, in many of the child abuse cases, the child was conceived out of wedlock. Bennie and Sclare (1969) report that the abused child was often the product of an unwanted pregnancy—the pregnancy was unwanted either because it was premarital or inconvenient. In Kempe et al.'s (1962) case #1 the battered child was an unwanted one, born soon after marriage "before the parents were ready for it." One of Resnick's (1969) cases of child murder reveals that a mother killed after she felt "labor pains" and was afraid she was pregnant again. The mother articulated the stress that another baby would cause by stating "how hard it is to raise even two children."

The finding that the abused child is often the product of an unwanted pregnancy ties in with the finding that the abused child is both young and usually the youngest or only child (Bennie and Sclare, 1969), and with Gil's (1971) finding that there is more abuse in families of four or more children. These findings suggest that a newborn, unwanted child may create a tremendous amount of stress in family life. The child may be a financial burden, an emotional burden, or a psychological burden to the parent or parents who did not plan or want the arrival. Thus, the unwanted child can become the receiver of a parent's aggression, not because of some fantasy or transference psychosis, but because the unwanted child is, in fact, a source of stress for the family. The abusive parents are *not* lashing out at a *projected* source of their troubles, they are beating a concrete source of family stress—an unwanted child.

The data about unemployment and unwanted children suggest that economic conditions producing stress and frustration are important factors in explaining parental abuse of children. This is a specific example of Goode's (1971) general proposition that a family that has little prestige, money, and power suffers greater frustration and bitterness and thus may resort to more violence (Goode, 1971).

Economic conditions are not the only source of stress that may lead to child abuse. Bennie and Sclare (1969) found that in four of seven cases of child abuse, women entered into marriage with men of different religions. The authors propose that intermarriage produced prolonged family stress, which eventually was a variable causing child abuse. Bennie and Sclare also found abusive families characterized by disrupted marital relationships. Zalba (1971) also found a great deal of marital and family conflicts in families where there were cases of child abuse.

THE CAUSES OF ABUSE: TOWARD A SOCIAL PSYCHOLOGICAL MODEL

That stress in the family is associated with child abuse is not a sufficient explanation of child abuse. In order to develop a broad causal model of child abuse, one would have to explain why abuse is an adaptation to stress—as opposed to other types of responses (Merton, 1938). This section extends the analysis of the causes of child abuse by examining the experience of parents with violence.

A review of the literature points out that abusive parents were raised in the same style that they have re-created in the pattern of rearing their own children (Steele and Pollock, 1968). Kempe et al. (1962) stated that attacking parents were subject to similar abuse as children, and that this pattern of child rearing is passed on in unchanged form. Gil's (1971) survey found that 11% of parents who abuse their children were victims of abuse during childhood. Granted, as the authors articulating the psychopathological approach argue, that abuse as a child had psychological consequences, it also has sociological consequences. One factor that determines what form of adaptation parents will use in dealing with family stress is their own childhood socialization. An individual who was raised by parents who used physical force to train

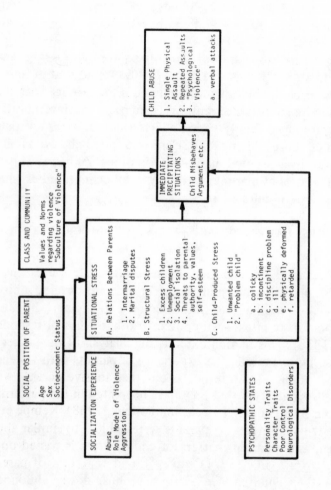

Figure 1: A Social Psychological Model of the Causes of Child Abuse

children and who grows up in a violent household has had as a role model the use of force and violence as a means of family problem-solving. The parents who re-create the pattern of abusive child rearing may be doing this because this is the means of child rearing they learned while growing up. It is the way they know of responding to stress and bringing up their child.

Considering this notion of child socialization and its effect on later patterns of child rearing, we may think of child abuse in terms of a social psychological model such as the one in Figure 1.

Some people would regard this model as the "social origins of psychopathology," and indeed the model does assume that a certain amount of child abuse is a function of psychopathic states (bottom left box). However, psychopathic states are only a possible, but not necessary, intervening variable in the explanation. The model goes beyond the unicausal approach by analyzing the sociocultural causes of abuse. The model assumes that frustration and stress are important variables associated with child abuse (middle box). Therefore, child abuse can be examined using the frustration-aggression approach (Miller, 1941). Certain structural conditions (Merton, 1938), such as social position, family roles, and unemployment (top left box and middle box) are also associated with abusive behavior towards children. In addition, norms concerning appropriate behavior and levels of physical punishment of children are important considerations (Wolfgang and Ferracuti, 1967) (top right box). Finally, the role of the child is important (middle and middle right box). The disposition of the child, the behavior, and the demands function as both causal factors and precipitating events of child abuse.

The purpose of presenting this model of factors influencing child abuse is not to suggest an exhaustive list of approaches nor to select one that is superior to the others. Instead, the purpose is to illustrate the complexity and the interrelationships of the factors that lead to child abuse.

CONCLUSION: IMPLICATIONS FOR STRATEGIES OF INTERVENTION AND FUTURE RESEARCH

When patients are diagnosed as sick, the treatment administered to them is designed to cure their illness. Consequently, when a child abuser is diagnosed as psychopath, the treatment is designed to cure the disease and prevent future episodes that result from the disease. Basically, the cure prescribed is psychological counseling, psychotherapy, psychoanalysis, psychiatric aid, and the other psychiatric mechanisms designed to rid the patient of the disorder. So far, the treatment of psychopathic disorders of abusive parents tends to be of limited effectiveness. Psychiatrists feel that treatment of the so-called sociopath or psychopath is rarely successful (Kempe et al., 1962). With this treatment being of limited utility, the only remaining strategy of intervention is to remove the child from the parents. Even this strategy has little success, because the state cannot keep the child from the parent indefinitely. Elmer (1967) reveals the case history of one family in which the child was abused, removed from the family, thrived, returned, and was again beaten.

Thus far, it seems that the existing strategies of intervention in child abuse cases hold little promise for solving the problem. This article suggests that one reason may be that the strategies are based on erroneous diagnoses of the problem. If one steps out of the psychopathological framework, it can be seen that the strategies are designed to cure symptoms that in many cases, do not exist. If the parent is not a psychopath in any meaningful sense of the word, then how can treatment aimed at eliminating the psychopathy be of consequence?

As far as developing new strategies of intervention, it is now necessary to stop thinking of child abuse as having a single cause: the mental aberrations of the parents. As Gil (1971) states, physical abuse of children is not a uniform phenomenon with one set of causal factors—but a multidimensional phenomenon. It is time to start thinking about the multiple social factors that influence child abuse. If unemployment and social class are important contextual variables, then strategies to prevent child abuse should aim at alleviating the disastrous effect of being poor in an affluent society. The fact that unwanted pregnancy appears so often in the cases indicates that programs ought to be designed to aid in planned parenthood, birth control devices, and the like. Within this area is also a strong argument for the removal of the legal and social stigma of abortion so that unwanted children do not have to be born. And, finally, because there appears to be an association between child rearing and child abuse, programs should be developed to teach parents alternative means of bringing up their children.

The major flaw that exists in current programs and current strategies of intervention is that they amount to an ambulance service at the bottom of the cliff. Child abuse programs now are after-the-fact treatment of parents and children. What needs to be done is to "fix the road on the cliff that causes the accidents." Strategies should be developed that can deal with the problem before the child is beaten or killed. These programs depend on a predictive theory of child abuse. The social psychological model of child abuse in this essay is a start in that direction.

NOTES

1. Not *all* students of child abuse subscribe to or support the psychopathological model. Two notable exceptions, who approach child abuse with a more multi-dimensional model are David Gil (1971) and Myra Blumberg (1964).

2. Similar problems of the psychopathological approach to child abuse are also articulated in sociological analyses of other forms of deviancy. See, for examples, Dunham (1964); Becker (1963); and Hakeem (1957).

3. This multidimensional approach has been advocated by Gil (1971) in his research on child abuse (see also, Gil, 1970 and Gil, D., 1966, "First steps in a nation-wide study on child abuse," *in* Social Work Practice, Columbia University Press, New York). Much of the material in this section is drawn from Gil's empirical research and theoretical formulations, which focus on social and economic factors related to child abuse.

4. There are a wide range of interpretations that can be applied to statistical data on child abuse (see Steinmetz and Straus, 1973a, notes 1 and 2 for detailed discussion of this). One problem in interpreting the data is that middle-class children might be overrepresented in the case literature, because their parents have more resources to draw on in obtaining medical and psychological attention for their children and themselves. On the other hand, middle-class children might be underrepresented because the act of child abuse might be more shocking to middle-class families, and lead them to use their resources to "cover up" the abuse by seeking help from a private physician or clinic.

Chapter 2

THE SOCIAL CONSTRUCTION OF CHILD ABUSE

During the last four years a great deal of attention has been focused on the problem of abused, battered, and murdered children. Numerous newspaper articles, television documentaries, and radio programs have been devoted to this social problem. In addition, the legal area of child abuse has undergone a radical change, with many states updating or instituting new laws on how best to deal with the phenomenon of children abused by their caretakers. The Mondale Bill, or Child Abuse Prevention and Treatment Act of 1973 (P.L. 93-247), has been implemented to attack the problem of abuse. On another front, the volume of attention received by the topic of child abuse is even more evident. The Department of Health, Education and Welfare published the *Bibliography on the Battered Child in 1969.* Since this bibliography was printed, the number of published articles, research reports, and books on child abuse has multiplied tenfold.[1] Whereas, Helfer and Kempe's *The Battered Child* (1968) was the major source book on child abuse in 1969,[2] there are now at least eight major works devoted to this topic (Bakan, 1971; Billingsley and Giovannoni, 1972; Decourcy and Decourcy, 1973; DeFrancis and Lucht, 1974; Fontana, 1971; Gil, 1970; Helfer and Kempe, 1972; Steinmetz and Straus, 1974).

In June 1973, the Department of Health, Education and Welfare authorized three million dollars for research on child abuse, and the National Institute for Child Development spent an additional $200,000 in 1974. Consequently, we can anticipate a continued rapid growth of the literature and research on child abuse.

We can break down current research on child abuse into three major areas; incidence, etiology, and prevention and treatment. The first major task that faced investigators of child abuse was to determine how extensive the phenomenon was. Estimates ranged from the 6,000 confirmed reported cases found by Gil (1970) to a half-million cases estimated by Light (1974), based on Gil's survey data. Other studies (Fontana, 1971; Heins, 1969; Newberger et al. 1973) attempted to assess the number of cases of child abuse in a given area, such as Boston or New York. At present, we can estimate that perhaps a half-million to a million children are abused by their caretakers each year.

A second phase of research on child abuse was a study of causes of abuse. Early studies using available case data proposed a psychopathological explanation of abuse (Galdston, 1965; Kempe et al., 1962; Steele and Pollock, 1968). However, these unicausal accounts were critically attacked as being too narrow and based on insufficient and inadequate data (Gelles, 1973; Gil, 1971, 1970.) However, even these new studies are being criticized through the use of better data and more refined data analysis techniques (Erlanger, 1974).

The last facet of work being done on child abuse concerns prevention and treatment of abused children and their parents (Helfer and Kempe, 1972). In addition to published accounts of treatment programs, we also have learned about other types of treatment and prevention programs, such as a self-help group, Parents Anonymous, formed by Jolly K. The future work in child abuse appears to be in the area of treatment and prevention. The aforementioned national child abuse bill authorized 60 million dollars, to be spent over the next three years, for developing programs to prevent and treat cases of child abuse.

Child Abuse as Social Deviance

There is one, as yet unrecognized, theme that runs throughout the study of child abuse, which has not been discussed but which pervades all the work and findings we have to date: child abuse is *social deviance*. Because child abuse is social deviance, all the cases that make up the data on incidence, all the explanatory analyses, and all the prevention and treatment models are influenced by the *social process* by which individuals and groups are labeled and designated as deviants. In other words, there is no objective behavior we can automatically recognize as child abuse.[3] An example is the definition of child abuse provided by the Child Abuse Prevention and Treatment Act of 1973:

> Child abuse and neglect means the physical or mental injury, sexual abuse, negligent treatment, or maltreatment of a child under the age of eighteen by a person who is responsible for the child's welfare under circumstances which indicate that the child's health or welfare is harmed or threatened thereby

While some parts of this definition are straightforward, there is a serious problem in determining what constitutes "mental injury," "negligent treatment," "maltreatment," "harm," or "threatened harm." While broken bones can be identified by X-ray, how can we identify a mental injury? Furthermore, if no bones are broken, who is to determine what is an injury and what is the routine use of physical punishment? The judges who develop a definition of child abuse, and the way they apply it, are of critical importance; as yet this phenomenon has not been studied.

Thus, when I speak of the social construction of abuse, I mean the process by which: (a) a definition of abuse is constructed; (b) certain judges or "gatekeepers" are selected for applying the definition; and (c) the definition is applied by designating the labels "abuse" and "abuser" to particular individuals and families.

This social process of defining abuse and labeling abusers should be an important facet in the study of child abuse. It should be a central issue because it affects all three main aspects of work in the area of abuse. First, how abuse is defined determines the extent of child abuse in America. If we confine our definition to one that calls abuse only those cases where *observable* physical injury has been *deliberately* caused by a caretaker, then our incidence of abuse will be comparatively small. If, on the other hand, we apply the definition provided by the Child Abuse Prevention and Treatment Act, the incidence of abuse may be as high as tens of millions of children (depending on what we call mental injury). Second, *who* gets labeled an abuser will drastically affect our conclusions about the etiology and causes of abuse. One reason the early analyses of the causes of child abuse were so inadequate and inaccurate was that they used only at-hand cases on which to base theories of causation. Thus, the factors which caused patients A, B, C, D, and the like to end up in Colorado Medical Center and then be labeled as cases of abuse were confounded in the causal explanation of abuse (not to mention the fact that being labeled an abuser by the hospital staff may have produced the personality characteristics—anxiety, depression, and the like—which were later called the causes of the abuse!). Finally, all these factors—defining abuse and selectively labeling certain people abusers—have profound implications on the strategies of intervention designed to prevent and treat abuse. Because of problems of definition and labeling, we may only be treating a very narrow portion of the true population of abusers and our treatment methods may be totally inadequate to deal with the unrecognized population of abusers and abused.

This analysis advances the theme of the social construction of child abuse by presenting a discussion of abuse using a theoretical framework developed by the labeling school of the sociology of deviance (Becker, 1963, 1964; Erickson, 1962; Lemert, 1951; Scheff, 1966). In addition, I shall outline the implications of this focus on socially constructed child abuse for present and future investigations into the area of child abuse.

The Social Construction of Child Abuse

The concept "child abuse" has had a wide variety of definitions applied to it, ranging from an occurrence where a caretaker injures a child, not by accident but in anger or deliberately (Gil, 1970) to "failure to thrive" (Bullard et al., 1967; Morris et al., 1964) to child theft, abandonment, or emotional mistreatment. Child abuse can be limited to a clinical condition, typically broken bones or physical trauma, which is determined by X-ray (this is the definition that Kempe et al. [1962] labeled the battered child syndrome), or child abuse can be a wide range of activities which include improper clothing, feeding, or caring for a child (Young, 1964).

Thus, a major problem in the area of child abuse is that of defining the phenomenon to be investigated. A corollary problem which arises is that it is impossible to compare the abundant data that have been gathered on abuse because of the idiosyncratic and varying definitions of child abuse.

A fundamental question, therefore, is, how do we deal with the problems of varying definitions of child abuse? One answer is that we make this very problem the subject of empirical investigation by introducing the theoretical perspective developed by the labeling school of social deviance.

LABELING AND SOCIAL DEVIANCE

The labeling school of deviance focuses its attention on the process by which individuals or groups become designated as deviants. Thus, for labeling theorists, deviance is not a property *inherent* in certain forms of behavior; it is a property *conferred upon* these forms by audiences which directly or indirectly witness the behavior in question (Erickson, 1962). The conferring of a label requires an audience or labeler, and it requires that a label be successfully applied. The successful application of a label of deviance is dependent on circumstances of the situation and place, the social and personal biographies of the labelers and the "deviant," and the bureaucratically organized activities of agencies of social control (Kitsuse, 1964).

The process of labeling is of critical importance to understanding how deviance is defined and how certain individuals become labeled as deviants. In terms of child abuse, this process or interaction can be seen in the confrontation between accused abusive parents and the accuser, be he neighbor, police, physician, or the court. It involves the accused "accounting" (Scott and Lyman, 1968) for what happened and the intricate "negotiation of identity" between the accused and the agents of authority (Scheff, 1966).

Rather than struggling for one uniform definition of child abuse, I propose that we investigate *who does the public labeling of abuse, what definitions or standards are employed, under what conditions are labels successfully applied, and what are the consequences of the labeling process.*

Gatekeepers. Of initial interest is the identification of those individuals or agencies that operate as the main gatekeepers in the process of labeling and defining a child as abused and a caretaker as an abuser. Research could focus on the flow of people, from the initial suspicion of abuse through the final gate of public labeling of abuser. It would be important to find out how cases of abuse are typically initiated. Are the parents the ones who report the abuse? Does a neighbor call the police? Where do social work and social service agencies fit in? We need to learn *who the gatekeepers are* who (1) initially attach the label of abuser to a caretaker, and (2) pass this individual through the "gate" and reinforce this label of abuser.

Definitions. Having identified the major labelers or gatekeepers, the next task would be to determine their definitions of abuse. Here it would be interesting to compare definitions of a neighbor, a policeman, a physician or nurse, a lawyer or court, a social worker or welfare worker. The importance of this information is that it provides an insight into why the incidence of reported abuse varies across and within particular social agencies. In addition, as we shall see in the following section, the definition of abuse influences who is labeled an abuser, and this in turn, influences the causal schemes that are developed to explain child abuse.

An examination of the generative sources of the varying definitions held by different gatekeepers would also help explain how and why different labels are attached to suspected abuse cases.

The Successful Labeling of Child Abuse. If we have identified the gatekeepers and their definitions, the next thing we need to know is how the gates operate and how the flow of people through agencies works to label some people abusers and other people nonabusers.

Polsky (1969) has pointed out that people who are caught in acts of deviance are systematically different from people who get away with the same acts (i.e., just getting caught indicates that they are "less" successful deviants). Thus, in the case of child abuse, our knowledge of who abuses a child, and why, is biased by the fact that the label of abuser is selectively applied.[4] The fact that labels are selectively applied mandates the study of the process of successful labeling of abusers and abused.

An important insight into the issue of successful labeling has been offered in the work of Sudnow (1964) and Simmons (1965). Sudnow's analysis of public defenders found that defenders' experience with criminal cases causes them to develop an occupational shorthand for "typing" crimes. They soon develop a knowledge of the routine grounds of different types of crime—who does them, what time of day, who the victims typically are, and the like. Simmons focused on the stereotypes of deviants held by people. These stereotypes were often unrelated to the actual actions considered deviant.

The same phenomenon that Sudnow calls "normal crime" is likely to occur in cases of child abuse. Policemen, physicians, nurses, and social workers who have either read literature on child abuse or had experience with child abuse cases, build up a mental inventory of characteristics of people and situations associated with child abuse. They "know" that abusers are typically poor and uneducated. Abused children are typically under three years of age. Mothers are more often abusers than are fathers. Thus, when they are presented with a case which is suspected of being abuse, they are likely to apply their previous experience and knowledge to determining whether or not this case is abuse. In short, if the literature states, or the practitioner's experience has been, that people who have certain personality traits are likely to abuse their children, and a person with those traits then shows up with an injured child, the practitioner would seem likely to label that person an abuser. Conversely, a person who arrives with an injured child, but does not fit the stereotype of abuse, may be more likely to avoid the label.

The previous discussion is only speculative. We need research that provides answers to the hypothesis that the label of abuse is differentially applied to individuals because of certain personal and social characteristics and certain aspects of the situation. Questions that could be answered through investigations which focus on the conditions of successful labeling are: To what degree does educational and occupational status insulate a person from being labeled as an abuser? What are the labelers' conceptions of the "routine grounds" of child abuse? On what are these conceptualizations based? Furthermore, we could begin to learn who abuses their child but does not get labeled an abuser. Information about how many individuals like this there are, and their personal and social characteristics, would go a long way towards refining and making more accurate our estimates of the incidence of child abuse and our causal models of child abuse.

Effects of Labeling. The last facet of studying child abuse by examining labeling and successful labeling is to assess the impact of the label "child abuser" on those individuals who have been successfully labeled abusers. Goffman (1963) has extensively analyzed the effects of labeling in his examination of "stigma." Other research has found that the effects of labeling vary, depending on the type of deviance alleged to have occurred and the social characteristics of the suspect (Schwartz and Skolnick, 1964).

By investigating the impact of the label abuser, we would be discovering what the effect of "becoming a child abuser" is on the personal, family, and social life of the accused. Earlier it was noted that the personality disorders commonly held to be the cause of child abuse may well be the *result* of being labeled an abuser.

In addition, the study of the effects of the label abuser would be a significant contribution to the creation and implementation of intervention programs designed to prevent and treat abuse. One reason why Parents Anonymous may be so successful is that the individuals involved do not have to suffer the stigma of public labeling. Conversely, the public screening process proposed by C. Henry Kempe, which could have firemen "screen" families for traits of potential abuse, may do more harm than good by subjecting upwards of a million Americans to the stigma of being falsely labeled a potential abuser (Light, 1974).

At least it ought to be recognized that the effects of being labeled an abuser may be more damaging to the individual caretakers and their children than is the actual instance of abuse. Research that uncovers information about the nature of this effect, and sensitizes us to its existence, would have a major influence on the design and implementation of prevention and treatment programs.

A Systems Approach to the Social Construction of Child Abuse

As a means of summing up these related issues, I propose a general framework within which the study of the social construction of child abuse can take place.

A glaring problem in the area of prevention and treatment of child abuse and other types of social problems is the lack of integration among the various agencies given the charge of dealing with the particular problem. Different agencies often approach the same problem at cross-purposes—many times at odds with each other, more frequently ignorant of what the other is doing. In the case of child abuse, a variety of agencies and agents encounter the problem and are called upon to make decisions. The medical profession is perhaps the most notable agency, because it has produced the majority of research findings and policy suggestions. The medical profession became involved in the area of child abuse when it found that it had a number of cases of physically injured children in which the evidence pointed to caretaker-inflicted injury. When Kempe et al. (1962) wrote his breakthrough essay on the battered child syndrome, he was actually pointing out a phenomenon that other pediatricians were aware of but, nevertheless, did not want to recognize. The Kempe essay made physicians and medical practitioners aware of the problem of child abuse, but none of this was new to other agencies, which had for years been trying to cope with the problem of abused children. Public and private social work agencies were well aware that many of their clients were either neglecting their children or physically abusing them. Policemen, the most frequent interveners in family disputes, also had firsthand knowledge of the problem. Teachers and guidance counselors also knew of cases of abused children. The courts were perhaps the most shielded from the problem because few of the other agents (policemen included) ever made official legal reports of the cases.

All of these agencies and agents have something to do with some part of the problem of child abuse. Each agency has its own gatekeepers, definitions of child abuse, and criteria for successful labeling; thus, each agency has a different impact on the suspected abuser. One way of beginning to integrate our knowledge about child abuse and our prevention and treatment programs is to take an overall view of the agencies involved in the problem. To do this I propose taking a social systems view of the various agencies, which perspective would employ the "open systems" framework (Katz and Kahn, 1966; Thompson, 1966) to explore the inter-actions and interface between the agencies.

At present, I see six systems involved in child abuse: the medical system (doctors, nurses, hospital administrators), the social service system (public and private agencies which provide ameliorative services to families and individuals), the criminal justice system (composed of police and the courts), the school system (teachers and counselors), the neighborhood and friend-ship system, and the family and kin system. All six social systems are involved in identifying, labeling, treating, and preventing child abuse. Therefore, in order to expand our knowledge of the label-ers—what are their definitions, how are their labels successfully applied, and how are we to best implement prevention and treat-ment programs?—we need to see how the entire system (made up of the six we have identified) operates. What are the interfaces between the various systems? How do people labeled abusers flow through the systems (one way, or back and forth)? How are people who abuse their children "lost" in the system, or unidenti-fied, and not given access to treatment programs? These I offer as some of the fundamental questions that need to be answered and that can be answered by taking a social systems view of the problem of child abuse.

Conclusion

The purpose here, and the rationale behind focusing on child abuse as a "socially constructed" phenomenon, has not been to offer a major new approach to child abuse. The issues to which I have addressed myself are not new to those people involved in the area of child abuse. My intention has been to elevate these issues from underlying assumptions into empirically problematic questions. I have offered this commentary as one way of breaking out of the endless definitional hassling about "what really causes abuse," and the shotgun approach to prevention and treatment programs. The issues raised here can serve as a foundation for future research that can and should have important implications for knowledge about child abuse as social behavior.

NOTES

1. This is a guess at the increase. The exact number of references listed in the 1974 NIMH bibliography on child abuse is 138.

2. Two other major books (Elmer et al., 1967; Young, 1964) were also available at this time, but neither was as explicit or detailed.

3. There are *some* cases that so clearly involve abuse that they are indeed automatically recognized. The literature abounds in cases where parents killed or cruelly tortured their children. I argue that there is no objective behavior which can be automatically labeled abuse, because these "outrageous" cases constitute a minor fraction of the overall number of incidents of a caretaker injuring a child.

4. Other methodological problems of child abuse research are noted by Gelles (1973) and Spinetta and Rigler (1972).

Chapter 3

COMMUNITY AGENCIES AND CHILD ABUSE:

LABELING AND GATEKEEPING

Although there is evidence that child abuse has been a part of family relations throughout recorded history (Bakan, 1971; De-Mause, 1975, 1974; Newberger and Hyde, 1975; Radbill, 1974), child abusers and abused children have been among the missing persons of both professional literature on the family and of social service agency programs. The last 10 years has seen a reversal in the trend of "selective inattention" (Dexter, 1958) to the problem of abuse and there is now a "knowledge explosion" in terms of literature and programs which focus on the abuse of children. This attention, while it may mislead some people into believing we are seeing a dramatic rise in the incidence and scope of abuse, has placed a great deal of pressure on those community agencies whose task it is to provide ameliorative services to families. These agencies find that they are called on to seek out and identify cases

From Richard J. Gelles, "Community Agencies and Child Abuse: Labeling and Gatekeeping." Presented at the Study Group on Recent Research on the Interaction Between the Family and Society, 1975. Ann Arbor: University of Michigan and Society for Research on Child Development.

of abuse (this active case seeking is a major contributor to the "dramatic rise" in child abuse incidence statistics), and to design and implement programs which treat abused children and their abusive caretakers.

The traditional ideology employed by the community agencies who come face to face with child abuse is that these agencies are *reactors* to the problem of abuse. This view sees abuse as a personal and family problem which requires individual and family services. As Paulson and Blake state, "the abusive father and mother represent a threat to the community" and it is the task of community agencies to "rehabilitate the parents" (1969: 93).

This essay proposes that agencies are far from simple *reactors* to social problems; rather, they play major and active roles in defining the nature and scope of the problem. Moreover, the definitions of the problem which they employ determine which cases are likely to be processed and which ones will be missed by these agencies.

Child Abuse: Incidence, Cause, and Prevention and Treatment

With the rapid increase in attention focused on the problem of child abuse, community agencies have been under pressure to formulate and institute programs and invervention strategies designed to prevent and treat child abuse. The first effort in developing programs began as a result of the groundbreaking work done by C. Henry Kempe and his colleagues. Kempe's article on the battered child syndrome published in 1962 alerted the medical profession to the possibility that a major cause of injuries and deaths in children was willfully inflicted injury administered by a parent or caretaker. The ability to diagnose these injuries was enhanced by technological developments in pediatric radiology which allowed pediatricians to identify previously inflicted injuries (Caffey, 1946, 1957; Silverman, 1953; Woolley and Evans, 1955; Gil, 1970). Once child abuse had captured the attention of a portion of the medical profession it was also identified as a problem by social workers (Elmer, 1967; Young, 1964).

The early works on child abuse focused mainly on estimating the incidence of child abuse and devoting a great deal of time to arguing that abuse was both a widespread and a serious problem in families. Once it had been established that abuse was indeed widespread,[1] the next task was to determine what the etiology of abuse was. The first writings on child abuse (see for example, Kempe et al., 1962; Steele and Pollock, 1974,; Zalba, 1971; Galdston, 1965), proposed a psychological model of the causes of abuse. This position was challenged by authors proposing that the available data was more supportive of a social psychological theory (Gil, 1970; Gelles, 1973). The recent work (see for example, Newberger et al., 1975) postulates a multidimensional theory drawing on both psychological and sociological factors to explain the causes of abuse.

Although the question of "cause" of child abuse is still the subject of debate, the recent thrust of work in the area of child abuse has been to design prevention and treatment programs. The Child Abuse Prevention and Treatment Act of 1973 (P.L. 93-237) allocated 60 million dollars for the study of child abuse. The bulk of the money is being spent in the development of prevention and treatment programs designed to cut down the estimated high number of cases of abuse per annum.

The effort to develop prevention and treatment modalities has yielded a number of programs which focus on various aspects of the suspected causes of abuse. A sampling of these programs reveals treatment modalities which emphasize behavior modification (Polakow and Peabody, 1975), a combination day care center and treatment center (Ten Broeck, 1974; Galdston, 1975), hospital programs designed to uncover and treat abuse (Wolkenstein, 1975), a community approach to preventing abuse (Lovens and Rako, 1975), the use of volunteers to treat abusive families (Hinton and Sterling, 1975), and a variety of other personal, familial, and community projects designed to either prevent the occurrence of abuse or to provide services to families once abuse has occurred.

Although the scope of these projects is quite variable, there is one underlying factor which cuts across all programs established by community agencies to treat abuse—that similarity is the conception that there is some objective category of behavior which we can designate and identify as child abuse. The assumption that there is an objective form of behavior which is abuse makes the role of community agencies a reactive one. By reactive, we mean that if the agency sees abuse as an objective phenomenon, then the agency's mandate is to provide some sort of service to counterbalance the problems which cause abuse to occur.

To accept this view of abuse as being an objective phenomenon and to accept the role of the agency as a reactive role, overlooks two important facets of child abuse. In the first place, there is no objective phenomenon which can be automatically recognized as child abuse (Gelles, 1975b). For a child to be diagnosed as abused and for a parent to be accused as an abuser, requires someone to observe a behavior or the consequences of a behavior and then categorize that behavior as abusive. The necessity of having someone label a phenomenon child abuse means that personal, social, and structural variables impinge on the process by which a suspected case of abuse becomes a confirmed case. There is evidence that selective labeling occurs in the diagnosis of abuse. Newberger and his colleagues state that there is a "preferential susceptibility of poor and minority children to receive the diagnosis child abuse and neglect while children of middle and upper-class families may be more often identified as victims of accidents" (1975). Given the assumption that there is *no* objective phenomenon of abuse, then the role of community agencies and the employees of these agencies becomes far more active. They develop their own operational definition of child abuse, they decide who is and who is not abused, and they prescribe the appropriate treatment or intervention procedure. It is to this point that the balance of the essay is addressed—an examination of the active role played by community agencies in interacting with suspected cases of abuse, and the consequences of the agencies' actions for their clients, for other families who may be abusive, for families who are not abusive, and for our own knowledge of the phenomenon which we call child abuse.

Community Agencies as Gatekeepers

Community agencies such as hospitals, health care clinics, schools, public social work agencies, private social work agencies, and the police play an active part in diagnosing and then labeling suspected cases of child abuse. Sanders (1972) states that there are still a large number of (abuse) cases that go unreported and it is the responsibility of public and private agencies to develop procedures which insure that cases will be reported. In Florida this responsibility was carried to its logical conclusion when the state (with federal assistance) instituted a statewide telephone number (using a WATS line which could be used at no charge to the caller) for reporting suspected cases of abuse. In the first two years (1971-1973) 48,814 cases were reported to the Florida Division of Family Services (Hurt, 1975: 13).[2]

In the course of receiving reports of suspected abuse over the telephone or in the course of the work activities of police, physicians, school teachers, and social workers, decisions must be made as to whether an injury or a condition reported or observed in a child is child abuse. The agencies which are confronted with suspected cases of abuse serve as gates and gatekeepers which either admit selected cases as abuse, or turn away cases as not being abuse. The actions of people staffing the gates determine who will become a child abuser and an abused child. The implications of these gatekeeping activities go beyond the simple designation of who is or is not an abuser/abused. It is apparent that our current level of knowledge about the causes of child abuse is heavily influenced by the process by which agencies diagnose and label cases child abuse. Throughout the early studies of child abuse (see, for example, Kempe et al., 1962; Galdston, 1965; Steele and Pollock, 1974) the causal analyses of child abuse were based on the at-hand cases in physicians', psychiatrists', or social workers' files. This led to the confounding of those variables which made certain people likely to be labeled child abusers with the variables which were causal factors in the act(s) of child abuse (e.g., Is low-socioeconomic status causally related to child abuse, or are people from the lower-socioeconomic groups more likely to be labeled child abusers?). Although current researchers have been alerted to the problem of generalizing about the causes of abuse from at-hand case data (see a critique of child abuse research by Spinetta and Rigler, 1972 for a discussion of methodological problems with research on child abuse), the central problem has not been rectified. For instance, a majority of the research projects on child abuse which are funded by the National Center on Child Abuse and Neglect (under funds provided by P.L. 93-237) have chosen to operationalize the concept child abuse by using all those cases which are found in the files of state agencies mandated by state laws to be central registries for child abuse (such as the Protective Services Division of state departments of welfare or social and rehabilitative services).

If we operationalize child abuse in this manner, knowledge about the causes of child abuse and suggestions concerning possible intervention strategies are strongly influenced by the actions of those agencies which serve as gatekeepers for suspected cases of child abuse.

Given the fact that agencies and their members are key gatekeepers in determining who is abused and play a major part in the social construction of knowledge about child abuse, it would be beneficial to turn our attention to the various factors and processes which influence the activities of community gatekeepers and determine what is child abuse and who are child abusers.

CHILD ABUSE AND OCCUPATIONAL IDEOLOGY

The subject of community agency gatekeeping and labeling has been partially addressed by Lena and Warkov's (1974) examination of occupational perceptions of child abuse and neglect and Viano's (1974) survey of attitudes toward child abuse among American professionals. Both studies report that the amount of knowledge and interest in the topic of child abuse varies by professional group. Viano found that many professionals were uninterested in the issue of abuse and uncooperative in dealing with the problem (1974:3). Nurses, social workers, clergy, and the police were the only professional groups who stated that they would get personally involved in an abuse case (1974:7). Viano found that educators avoid personal involvement with abuse (1974:7-8). Lena and Warkov's investigation of occupational perceptions focused on how child abuse was defined and the factors which professionals felt were important causal variables in instances of child abuse. Lena and Warkov concluded that there was a fair degree of similarity between occupational groups on what constitutes abuse (1974:7). They went on to propose that professional groups share a perception or "occupational ideology" (Caplow, 1964) of the social problem of child abuse (1974:9).

The similarity of definitions of abuse found by Lena and Warkov is probably due to the fact that they sampled their respondents at seminars on child abuse, and it is likely that only those professionals already interested or informed on the topic of child abuse attended the seminars. Viano's findings that perceptions vary between professional groups probably portrays a more accurate picture of the outlook on child abuse held by community agencies.

Based on the work already done on occupational and professional perceptions of child abuse and on our own research on the social construction of child abuse (Gelles, 1975b states the basic theoretical position of this research), an initial proposition might be that *the occupational and organizational mandate of a community agency determine how active it will be in identifying cases of child abuse, how likely the employees of the agency are to label particular cases abuse, and the ·type of cases which are labeled child abuse.*

It is clear that an agency which does not see itself responsible for providing services to families suspected of child abuse and agencies who do not see it as their responsibility to locate cases of child abuse will simply not locate many cases. They may either overlook cases (i.e., classify a broken arm or leg as an accident), or they may label only those cases which they see as their agency's prime priority. An example of the former strategy of overlooking child abuse was found among physicians. A plastic surgeon who was questioned about his willingness to report suspected child abuse cases stated flatly that "I'm not a detective, that is not my job." It was clear that he meant that he viewed his mandate as being restricted to plastic surgery and that the cause of the condition which required the surgery was not in his occupational or professional domain. In another instance, a physician specializing in internal medicine completely overlooked evidence from an X-ray series that revealed numerous healed fractures of the arms and ribs. He referred the case to another service in the hospital without a mention of the possible causes of the fractures or the likelihood that he was treating a case of child abuse. An example of the latter phenomenon of selective perception of child abuse also is seen in the actions of physicians and hospitals. Research on child abuse done in hospital settings typically reports very few cases of child neglect (nonphysical injury). It is possible that child neglect cases do seek treatment from physicians and emergency rooms in hospitals; however, those physicians who are trained to identify child abuse typically equate abuse to physical injury or trauma (for instance, Kempe et al.'s essay in 1962 which opened up the area of child abuse for the medical profession restricted the definition of child abuse to physical trauma and injury). Social work agencies, by virtue of their training, occupational mandate, and diagnostic equipment and experience, are far more likely to diagnose cases of child neglect than child abuse (e.g., social workers do not have the benefit of X-ray technology to assist their diagnosis).

OCCUPATIONAL POWER AND LABELING

Viano discovered that the professional group which was least likely to become personally involved with child abuse was educators. The clergy was found to be somewhat timid in its willingness to be involved, social workers were split in their opinion, and the professional group which stated they would plunge headlong into the problem was the police (1974:8). Our discussions with educators (teachers and counselors), social workers, and physicians indicated that there were differences in willingness to get involved in reporting cases of child abuse in these professions. Interestingly, educators reported that they suspected large numbers of their pupils as being abused, but they had little desire to report abuse cases (thus, violating state law which mandates reporting). One explanation of why educators are so reluctant to get involved and why police, and to a certain extent physicians, are more likely to report cases of abuse is occupational power.[3] We propose that *the higher the occupational power, the more likely a member of that occupation is to report a suspected case of child abuse.* Physicians possess high occupational power by virtue of their prestigious position in the occupational hierarchy. The policeman's occupational power derives from his position as a law enforcer and the fact that he is a member of the only profession permitted to carry a weapon and use legitimate violence to enforce laws and rules. At the other end of the continuum, educators have a low degree of power because they are employees of the community who are delegated a narrow jurisdiction over the behavior of children and families. Teachers and counselors are aware of their low power in the community and are quite reluctant to offend the school board or parents by initiating child abuse reports.

PROFESSIONAL-CLIENT RELATIONS

A number of examinations of occupations and professions have focused on the complex relations which occur between client and professional (see Freidson, 1960; and Goffman, 1961 for examples). These relationships are crucial in determining the structure and nature of the professional relationship. In the case of child abuse we find that the degree of personal relations between the agency worker and the suspected case of abuse strongly influences how likely the agency is to report a client as an abuser and implement programs designed to treat and prevent abusive acts. Physicians report that they are more likely to report a case of child abuse in the course of their work in clinics or emergency rooms than in their private practice. A House Officer on a pediatrics service stated:

> Given the same condition or injury, a child who is seen in an emergency room is five times more likely to be diagnosed as abused than a child who is seen in a private practice.

Physicians and social workers report that they are much more reluctant to suspect abuse and neglect in families where they have established an enduring relationship. The fact that the more impersonal the relationship, the more chance there is that abuse will be observed and reported may partially explain Viano's finding that police are more likely to become involved in cases of abuse while the clergy and educators are much more timid in their involvement (1974).

The aspect of professional-client relations is evident in the problems encountered by educators in their interaction with suspected cases of child abuse. Educators typically are drawn into suspected cases of abuse either by observing injuries in their students or when the students confide to the educator that their parents or caretakers are abusing them. Teachers, counselors, and principals are thrust into the role of possible "double agents" if they use their observations or the reports they receive from their students as evidence in a reported child abuse case. Educators are torn between their legal responsibility to report abuse and the possibility that if they report a case they will erode the trust that students place in them when they seek counseling or guidance.

The more typical resolution of this dilemma is that educators rarely report suspected child abuse cases.

"Normal" Child Abuse

The previous section outlines some factors which influence which agencies are likely to deal with child abuse, what types of child abuse or neglect they focus on, and what factors influence their decision to report a case of child abuse. In this section we would like to explore the types of individuals who are "caught" abusing their children and then examine what factors cause particular individuals and families to be vulnerable to the label child abuser.

Newberger and his colleagues have pointed out that there is a preferential susceptibility of poor and minority children to receive the diagnosis of child abuse and neglect (1975). We would propose that *given similar conditions of the child, community agencies are more likely to label families with socially marginal status (ethnic outgroups, low-socioeconomic status, low power) as child abusers, while labeling families with greater prestige and status as having children who are victims of accidents.* This proposition stands as a plausible rival to the one which states that there is a causal association between social and economic marginality and child abuse. While we tend to agree with the latter hypothesis (see Gelles, 1973), we also are inclined to follow the lead of Horowitz and Liebowitz (1967) who state that social deviance and political marginality are closely associated—in other words, those people who are low in political and social power are most likely to be labeled society's deviants. It appears that the "poor are public" in the sense that their behavior is much more open to public scrutiny and public intervention. Because of this, they may be more vulnerable to the designation of abused/abuser.

DISCOVERING CASES

The literature on child abuse is in almost total agreement on one basic point, the most difficult task facing community agencies is that of uncovering, discovering, and investigating suspected cases of child abuse (Sanders, 1972). This is perhaps due to two facts; first, the family is society's most private institution (Laslett, 1973), thus most abusive behavior occurs in the privacy of the home, and second, the portrait of the child abuser-as-psychopath is so heinous a picture that it may motivate many families to cover-up all but lethal instances of abuse.

To reach the population of abusers who are defined as requiring social services, agencies develop a variety of strategies to investigate cases of suspected abuse. These strategies become the standard social screening techniques by which cases of abuse are uncovered.

One technique used by community agencies is to apply their standard of parent-child relations to the behavior they observe between their client and the client's child. We spoke to a pediatrician who informed us that the case she reported as abuse was detected when she noticed that an injured child was quite distant from his mother and quite friendly with the physician. This was in stark contrast to the typical situation pediatricians experience when children resist the doctor and cling to the parent. This pediatrician used her previous experience with children to detect an abnormality which she associated with abuse.

The second example is provided by Paulson and Blake (1969) who advise that effective diagnoses of child abuse can be accomplished if the attending physician looks for discrepancies between the nature and extent of the child's injury and the history of that injury provided by the accompanying person (see also Kempe et al., 1962 for the same advice to physicians). Newberger and Hyde (1975) illustrate this procedure when they describe a case where a massive hematoma overlying the left eye of a 10 month old was accounted for by the parent as being caused by a broom which, almost in defiance of the laws of physics and gravity, was propelled by the mother's foot in the baby's crib where it struck the child.

Thus, the social screening devices used by community agencies makes use of yardsticks of normal parent-child interaction and perceived deviations from these yardsticks as indicators of possible abuse, and the accounts (Lyman and Scott, 1970) used by parents to explain injuries. This indicates that the physical condition of the child is a necessary but not sufficient criterion for the diagnosis.

INVESTIGATING CASES

As in the case of discovering cases of child abuse, certain screening processes are used during the investigation phase of child abuse detection. In most instances where a case of child abuse is suspected, the community agency investigates the case, either by interviewing the suspect or visiting the family. The interviews with suspected abusive parents are typically guided by the agency's knowledge and reading on the subject of child abuse. Many social work agencies make use of Helfer and Kempe's book, *Helping the Battered Child and His Family* (1972). These agencies use the personal interview to screen families for the various social and psychological factors which are considered to be causal factors in acts of child abuse. Other agencies may make use of various writings on child abuse, or may make use of the agency's previous experience with abuse cases.

The most interesting screening devices are employed by agencies in the course of home visits. We have interviewed (informally) a number of private and public social workers and a surprising consistency emerges in their discussion of home visits to suspected cases of child abuse. We learned that the smell of urine and feces are prime indicators of the likelihood of child abuse occurring in a family. Agency workers who have investigated child abuse frequently describe the home as disorganized, with no set time for meals, children running around with tattered or no clothing, and the powerful smell of urine and feces striking the worker as s(he) enters the home.

There are a number of other factors, which vary by agency, which are used to identify child abuse. The medical agencies typically screen families by looking for premature births, difficult deliveries, and developmental abnormalities in children. Social work agencies are more keenly aware of familial organization and structural components such as single parent families and patterns of delivering meals to family members. Educators, unlike other agencies, have to rely on the accounts by the children to learn about child abuse. Thus, teachers, counselors, and school administrators depend on the accounts offered by the alleged victims of child abuse.

"NORMAL" ABUSE

The result of the techniques used to develop screening procedures for discovering and investigating cases of child abuse and the
experience gained as a result of these discoveries and investigations
produce a normal picture of child abuse, in the minds of the
workers in community agencies (see Sudnow, 1964 for discussion
of the idea of normal deviance as viewed by those individuals who
interact with deviants). Each community agency develops a stereo-
typed or normal portrait of the typical abuser, the typical family
in which abuse takes place, the circumstances which produce
abuse, the time of day, day of week, and time of the year abuse
occurs. These portraits become an occupational shorthand by
which agencies can expedite their discovery, investigation, and
provision of services to families labeled abusive. While these techniques are almost inevitable in the course of human interaction,
and are often efficient, they have unintended consequences which
we shall discuss in the concluding section of this essay.

Community Agency Gatekeeping: Consequences

One of the more obvious consequences of community agency
gatekeeping is the fact that whatever screening and investigation
devices are used, agencies are going to make mistakes in their
diagnoses of abuse. In short, agencies are going to not only
discover cases of child abuse, they are also going to have a number
of false positives (cases labeled abuse which are not) and false
negatives (cases not labeled abuse which are). To illustrate this
point, let us assume that a screening device was established for use
by all community agencies which would diagnose child abuse with
a 99% level of accuracy. And, let us assume that this device was
used by all community agencies to screen 100 million individuals
over the age of 18 for signs of abuse. If there are 10,000 cases of
abuse a year in the United States, this technique is going to
uncover most of these cases. However, using this technique will
also mean that one million families will be labeled abusive by
mistake (see Light, 1974 for the statistical procedure used in
coming up with these figures).

Thus, using a very precise screening technique we are going to
(1) spend a great deal of time and money providing services to

families which do not require them, and (2) we are going to subject one million families to the stigma and damage of being falsely labeled child abusers.

The illustration which we provided is not particularly realistic (because neither the screening device, nor the procedure for screening all families exist), but there is a point to be made by this illustration. It articulates the basic problem which must be addressed by community agencies in their interaction with suspected cases of child abuse. Each agency must make the pragmatic and philosophic decision as to how aggressive it will be in seeking cases of child abuse. In other words, what type of "error" does it want to make—missing cases or falsely accusing families. At this point in time, given the social constraints imposed by agency and occupational power and the sensitivity of interpersonal relations, it appears that most agencies are willing to accept false negatives to protect themselves from the consequences of false positive diagnoses.

THE AGENCY "WALTZ"

In the course of interviewing members of 80 families on the subject of intrafamilial violence (Gelles, 1974), we spoke with a number of people who had prolonged interaction with community agencies and who had histories of high physical violence between husband and wife and parent to child. One of the more interesting findings derived from these interviews was that we learned that despite the fact that many of these families could have been reported as abusing their children, none were. The families explained that they really had not made much of an attempt to conceal the fact that they had injured a child with physical punishment. They seemed to be concerned that they had never received much help from the agency, and this was in part due to what one woman called "the agency waltz." The agency waltz was, as our respondent described it, a technique used by agencies to get people the kind of services they desired. What happens is that a parent goes to an agency with a single complaint, but in the course of the intake interview other problems are discussed. The agency then refers the family to another agency more qualified to deal with the total range of problems. This agency refers the family to a third or fourth agency. By this time, only the most persistent families are left in the system, the rest having fallen between the seams of the social service system as a consequence of the agency waltz.

The fact that there are numerous private and public agencies delegated the task of providing basic and needed services to families is the result of political, economic, and social processes which we are not qualified to discuss. However, we have seen the consequences of this system, and the consequences are that the decentralized system of human services results in many cases of child abuse falling away from the social service system. The newspapers often report cases of fatal incidents of child abuse where the police, courts, and social agencies all knew about the family's history of child abuse, but where no agency had taken the responsibility to do anything.

The gatekeeping process, combined with multiple agencies and multiple agency mandates means that many if not most cases of child abuse will go undetected and without services.

THE SERVICES PROVIDED

There is little doubt that community agencies do help many or even most of their clients. In the case of child abuse, there are reports of various intervention procedures and strategies working "wonders" with abusive families. Almost every agency and every agency worker can point to particular cases which were aided through community agency intervention. We will not, nor can we, dispute these achievements. But we can point out that the particular ways programs are set up by community agencies, are located in the community, and staffed, determine which type of individual is likely to be identified, treated, and treated successfully. The person who brings a child to a medical center and confides in a doctor is systematically different from an individual who seeks private family counseling for an abuse problem and from an individual who is identified by a social work agency. Thus, in most cases, services provided by agencies are client-specific—they work for particular clients and are dismal failures with others. The clients who do not "thrive" under agency programs either move to another agency (the agency waltz revisited) or drop away from the agency system. Agencies are like social "magnets," they repel as well as attract cases. This being the case, the services provided are derived as a result of the complex series of interactions between agencies and clients which determine what kinds of problems the agency will deal with and what kinds of clients they will interact with.

Implications for Social Policy

This essay has reviewed the subject of community agency labeling and gatekeeping of cases of child abuse. We have discussed the gatekeeping role played by community agencies and have identified a number of factors which influence the activities of community gatekeepers and determine what cases of child abuse will be diagnosed. Finally, the essay briefly discussed some of the consequences of agency gatekeeping.

The concluding section of the essay focuses on some policy implications which can be inferred from a review of the gatekeeping and labeling activities of community agencies.

WHO SHALL BE PROTECTED?

It is clear that despite good intentions and training, community agencies will make errors of diagnosis in screening children and families for child abuse. As the definition of child abuse is broadened to include such things as "mental injury" and "psychological abuse," the error factor in diagnosing suspected cases will increase. While X-rays can detect current and previous physical abuse, no such technology exists for diagnosing mental or psychological abuse.

Second, as the definition of child abuse is broadened, the cost of screening cases is increased. More attention must be paid to the parents, children, and home environment if the subtle symptoms of nonphysical abuse are to be recognized.

It might be wise for community agencies to determine which children are at greatest risk, and strive to protect them as well as possible. By identifying the most seriously at-risk children, agencies can reduce the error factor in diagnosis to a manageable level, and also provide direct services to children and families within reasonable budgetary constraints. While, in an ideal world, it would be desirable to protect all children and guarantee them the right to a risk-free childhood, it is simply not within our knowledge or resources to protect all children who might be physically, sexually, or psychologically abused.

AGENCY COOPERATION

The idiosyncratic methods used by agencies to diagnose and treat suspected cases of child abuse often put abused children and abusive parents on a never ending merry-go-round of agency visits. Although child abuse research has revealed abuse as a phenomenon with multiple causes, the multidimensional theory has not yet been translated into agency practice. There is a desperate need for more interagency cooperation, both in diagnosing and in treating cases of abuse.

INFORMATION CONTROL

The groundbreaking research on child abuse revealed a problem that went on under the eyes of the medical and social service profession. In many instances, cases of abuse went unnoticed because abusive parents would "hospital-hop" with their children. Thus, each admission of an injured child came with no prior medical or social history. Physicians and hospital social workers were often unable to determine if the injury was the result of an idiosyncratic event, or was part of an ongoing pattern of abuse. To improve on diagnosing cases of abuse, states instituted central clearinghouses for child abuse reports. These clearinghouses offered physicians and social workers information on their clients which they could use to determine if a child had been abused.

Although these clearinghouses are beneficial, they pose a clear and serious danger to the families who have been reported as child abusers. If the clearinghouses do not update and clean their files on confirmed and nonconfirmed cases of abuse, many families run the risk of being permanent falsely identified cases of abuse. The potential for misuse of these clearinghouse files becomes evident when reports are issued that juvenile delinquents are found to have been abused as children. One can easily foresee a situation where child abuse clearinghouse records are used to monitor children

from infancy to their teens, looking for the first signs of delinquency. A graver misuse of the records could come if law enforcement agencies could use child abuse records as means of screening
suspects for crimes. Clearly, the data which we collect on *suspected* cases of child abuse must be collected, maintained, and
used in a manner which protects individuals and families from
gross infringements on their personal rights.

NOTES

1. "Established" should be interpreted with the *caveat* that it has not been empirically established exactly what the incidence of child abuse is.

2. The ability to uncover cases of child abuse produced more problems than it solved
for the state of Florida. In the first place, the state did not have the financial or
programmatic resources to follow up each and every report. Second, the level of
knowledge about child abuse, its causes and solutions, was, and is still, not advanced
enough for the state to provide ameliorative services to all those callers requesting it for
themselves or others.

3. This willingness to get involved varies despite state law which protects all occupations and all individuals reporting child abuse from criminal or civil prosecution.

Chapter 4

VIOLENCE TOWARD CHILDREN IN THE UNITED STATES

This essay reports on the incidence, modes, and patterns of parent-to-child violence in the United States. Despite the considerable attention that has been focused on the issue of child abuse and neglect, and the significant and lengthy discussions concerning the physical punishment of children, valid and reliable data on the incidence and prevalence of the use of violence and aggression on children by their parents are almost nonexistent. The statistics that are available on child abuse and physical punishment do not report on the numerous violent acts that are neither routine physical punishment nor abusive. The wide range of acts between spankings and grievous assault have largely gone unnoticed and unresearched by social scientists.

Available data are often flawed by conceptual, definitional, sampling, and measurement problems. Moreover, the available statistics are usually general estimates of incidence which do not give even the crudest breakdown by age, sex, or demographic

Reprinted, with permission, from the American Journal of Orthopsychiatry. Copyright 1978 by the American Orthopsychiatric Association, Inc.

characteristics of the children or parents. Nevertheless, the figures on violence and aggression between parents and children do shed *some* light on the scope of the phenomenon.

PHYSICAL PUNISHMENT

The most comprehensive research on the use of physical force on children are the studies of physical punishment. Between 84% and 97% of all parents use some form of physical punishment on their children (Blumberg, 1964; Erlanger, 1974; Stark and Mc-Evoy, 1970). The advantage of these data is that they are typically based on nationally representative surveys. The disadvantages are that they do not provide age-specific rates nor do they examine specific acts of force.

CHILD ABUSE

A variety of research strategies have been employed to investigate the incidence of child abuse in America.

Official statistics. Investigations of official reports of child abuse provide varying degrees of the yearly incidence of abuse. Gil's 1968 survey yielded a figure of 6,000 abused children (1970). One problem with the Gil survey is that all 50 states did not have mandatory reporting laws for the period Gil studied. The Children's Division of the American Humane Society documented 35,642 cases of child abuse in 1974, which were reported to its clearinghouse for child abuse and neglect reports (American Humane Association, 1974). However, only 29 states reported to the clearinghouse.

Estimates derived from official reports suffer from various problems. First, official reports do not cover all possible states and localities. Second, states and localities do not employ uniform definitions of child abuse. Third, official reports represent only a fraction of the total number of children who are abused and battered by their parents.

Household surveys. In 1965, the National Opinion Research Corporation and David Gil collaborated on a household survey of attitudes, knowledge and opinions about child abuse. Of a nationally representative sample of 1,520 individuals, 45, or 3% of the sample, reported knowledge of 48 different incidents of child abuse. Extrapolating this finding to the national population, Gil estimated that between 2.53 and 4.07 million adults knew of families involved in incidents of child abuse (Gil, 1970). Light (1974), by applying corrective adjustments to Gil's data and considering possible overlap of public knowledge of incidents, revised the estimate to be approximately 500,000 abused children in the United States during the survey year.

Survey of community agencies. Nagi (1975) attempted to compensate for the shortcoming of estimates of child abuse based on official records by surveying a national sample of community agencies and agency personnel to ascertain how many cases of child abuse they encountered annually. Nagi's estimate of child abuse was arrived at by extrapolating from reporting rates which would be expected on a national basis using presumed "full reporting rates" found in Florida. Nagi's estimate is that 167,000 cases of abuse are reported annually, while an additional 91,000 cases go unreported (1975).

Statistical projection. Estimates of the incidence of child abuse have also been based on projections from regional, state, city, or single agency samples. The range of these estimates is quite wide. DeFrancis estimated that there are between 30,000 and 40,000 instances of "truly battered children" each year (U.S. Senate, 1973). Fontana (1973) proposed that there may be as many as 1.5 million cases of child abuse each year. Kempe (1971) set the figure closer to 60,000 cases. Cohen and Sussman (1975) used data on reported child abuse from the 10 most populous states and projected 41,104 confirmed cases of child abuse in 1973.

DEATHS OF CHILDREN BY VIOLENCE

Just as estimates of the incidence of child abuse vary, so do estimates of the number of children killed each year by parents or guardians. Fontana (1973) provided a conservative estimate of 700 children killed each year. Helfer (U.S. Senate, 1973) has stated that, if steps are not taken to curb child abuse, there will be over 5,000 deaths a year over the next 10 years. *Pediatric News* (1975) reported that one child dies each day from abuse—a yearly incidence of 365. Gil (1970) cited data from the U.S. Public Health Service, which reported 686 children under 15 died from attacks by parents in 1967.

SUMMARY OF RESEARCH

Perhaps the most accurate summary of the research on the incidence and extent of child abuse is provided by Cohen and Sussman (1975), who concluded that:

> the only conclusion which can be made fairly is that information indicating the incidence of child abuse in the United States simply does not exist.

It is evident that most projections of the incidence of child abuse are "educated guesses." Information gleaned from official statistics must be qualified by the fact that they represent only caught cases of abuse, which become cases through varied reporting and confirmation procedures (Gelles, 1975b). In addition, information on child abuse is difficult to interpret because the term child abuse is as much a political concept (designed to draw attention to a social problem) as it is a scientific concept that can be used to measure a specific phenomenon. In other words, child abuse can be broadly and loosely defined in order to magnify concern about this social problem. While some social scientists use the term to cover a wide spectrum of phenomena that hinder the proper development of a child's potential (Gil, 1975), others use the term to focus attention on the specific case of severely physically injured children (Kempe et al., 1962).

The lack of valid and reliable data on the incidence of child abuse in the United States led to the inclusion of a clause in the Child Abuse Prevention and Treatment Act of 1974 (P.L. 93-237) calling for a full and complete study on the incidence of child abuse and neglect. Such a study has already been contracted by the National Center on Child Abuse and Neglect. As an indication of the major problems that arise when one tries to measure the abuse and neglect of children, the contracted study has moved into the third quarter of its two-year existence and no decisions have been made on appropriate definitions of abuse or what research design should be employed in the study.

A NOTE ON TREND DATA

It should be pointed out that the problems involved in estimating the incidence of child abuse make the task of interpreting trend data almost hopeless. First, it is impossible to determine if rates of reported abuse are rising due to an actual increase in the true rate of abuse or due to increased sensitivity on the part of professionals who see children and families. Second, the constant change in the definition of abuse and the constant revisions of state child abuse and neglect laws, tend to broaden the definition of child abuse. This means that more families and children are vulnerable to being identified as abusers and abused.

THE NEED FOR A STUDY OF PARENTAL VIOLENCE

It was after evaluating the available evidence on the extent of force and violence between parents and children that we embarked on a national study of parental and family violence. While physical punishment of children appears to be almost a universal aspect of parent-child relations, and while child abuse seems to be a major social problem, we know very little about the modes and patterns of violence toward children in our society. We know almost nothing about the kinds of force and violence children experience. Are mothers more likely than fathers to hit their children? Who employs the most serious forms of violence? Which age group is most vulnerable to being spanked, slapped, hit with a fist, or "beaten up" by parents? Although answers to these questions will not completely fill in the gaps in our knowledge about child abuse, we see the information we generate in this study as providing an important insight into the extent of force and violence children experience and the numbers of children who are vulnerable to injury from serious violence.

Method

One of the most difficult techniques of studying the extent of parental violence is to employ a household interview that involves the self-reporting of violent acts. Although this technique is difficult and creates the problem of underreporting, we felt that, because of the shortcomings of previous research on child abuse (Gelles, 1978a), this was the only research design we could employ to assess the extent and causes of intrafamily violence.

SAMPLE AND PROCEDURES

Response Analysis (Princeton, NJ) was contracted to draw a national probability sample. A national sample of 103 primary areas (counties or groups of counties) stratified by geographic region, type of community, and other population characteristics was generated. Within these primary areas, 300 interviewing locations (census districts or block groups) were selected. Each location was divided into 10 to 25 housing units by the trained interviewers. Sample segments from each interviewing location were selected. The last step involved randomly selecting an eligible person to be interviewed in each designated household.

Eligible families consisted of a couple who identified themselves as married or being a "couple" (man and woman living together in a conjugal unit). A random procedure was used so that the sample would be approximately half male and half female.

The final national probability sample produced 2,143 completed interviews.[1] Interviews were conducted with 960 men and 1,183 women. In each family where there was at least one child living at home between the ages of 3 and 17, a "referent child" was selected using a random procedure. Of the 2,143 families interviewed, 1,146 had children between the ages of 3 and 17 living at home. Our data on parent-to-child violence are based on the analysis of these 1,146 parent-child relationships.

The interviews were conducted between January and April 1976. The interview protocol took 60 minutes to complete. The questions on parent-to-child violence were one part of an extensive protocol designed to measure the extent of family violence and the factors associated with violence between family members.

VIOLENCE: DEFINED AND OPERATIONALIZED

For the purposes of this study, violence is nominally defined as "an act carried out with the intention, or perceived intention, of physically injuring another person." The injury can range from slight pain, as in a slap, to murder. The motivation may range from a concern for a child's safety (as when a child is spanked for going into the street) to hostility so intense that the death of the child is desired (Gelles and Straus, 1979).

We chose a broad definition of violence (which includes spankings as violent behavior) because we want to draw attention to the issue of people hitting one another in families; we have defined this behavior as "violent" in order to raise controversy and call the behavior into question. In addition, our previous research (Gelles, 1974) indicated that almost all acts, from spankings to murder, could somehow be justified and neutralized by someone as being in the best interests of the victim. Indeed, one thing that influenced our final choice of a concept was that acts parents carry out on their children in the name of corporal punishment or acceptable force, could, if done to strangers or adults, be considered criminal assault.

Violence was operationalized in our study through the use of a Conflict Tactics Technique scale. First developed at the University of New Hampshire in 1971, this technique has been used and modified extensively since then in numerous studies of family violence (Allen and Straus, 1975; Bulcroft and Straus, 1975; Straus, 1974b). The Conflict Tactics Technique scales were designed to measure intrafamily conflict in terms of the means used to resolve conflicts of interest (Straus, 1979c). The scale used contains 18 items in three groups: (1) use of rational discussion and argument (discussed the issue calmly; got information to back up your side; brought in/tried to bring in someone to help settle things), (2) use of verbal and nonverbal expressions of hostility (insulted or swore at the other; sulked or refused to talk about it; stomped out of room or house; cried, did or said something to spite the other; threatened to hit or throw something at other; threw, smashed, hit, or kicked something), and (3) use of physical force or violence as a means of managing the conflict (threw something at the other; pushed, grabbed, shoved the other; slapped or spanked; kicked, bit, or hit with a fist; hit or tried to hit with something; beat up the other; threatened with a knife or gun; used knife or gun).[2]

Administration of the Conflict Tactics Technique involves presenting the subjects with the list of 18 items, in the order enumerated above, and asking them to indicate what they did when they had a disagreement with the referent child in the past year and in the course of their relationship.

Reliability and validity. The reliability and validity of the Conflict Tactics Technique has been assessed over the five-year period of its development and modification. Pretests on more than 300 college students indicated that the indices have an adequate level of internal consistency reliability (Straus, 1979c). Bulcroft and Straus (1975) provided evidence of concurrent validity. In addition, evidence of "construct validity" exists, in that data compiled in the pretests of the scale are in accord with previous empirical findings and theories (Straus, 1979c).

Advantages and disadvantages of the violence scale. An advantage of the violence scale, aside from previous evidence of its reliability, "concurrent" validity, and "construct" validity, is that the mode of administration increased the likelihood of the interviewer establishing rapport with the subject. The eight force and violence items came at the end of the list of conflict tactics. Presumably, this enhanced the likelihood that the subject would become committed to the interview and continue answering questions. Our analysis of the responses to the items indicates that there was no noticeable drop in the completion rate of items as the list moved from the rational scale questions to the most violent modes of conflict management.

Two disadvantages of the scale are that it focuses on conflict situations and does not allow for the measurement of the use of violence in situations where there was no "conflict of interest," and that it deals with the *commission* of acts only. We have no idea of the *consequences* of those acts, and thus have only a limited basis for projecting these statistics to the extent of the phenomenon child abuse, because child abuse normally is thought to have injurious consequences for a child. While we may learn that a parent used a gun or a knife, and we can presume that this has negative consequences for a child, even if the child was not injured, we do not know what the actual consequences were.

Results

As proposed at the outset of this essay, "ordinary" physical punishment and child abuse are but two ends of a single continuum of violence toward children. In between are millions of parents whose use of physical force goes beyond mild punishment, but for various reasons does not get identified and labeled as child abuse.

Of the respondents, 63% who had children between the ages of 3 and 17 living at home mentioned at least one violent episode during the survey year (1975). The proportion of our sample reporting at least one violent occurrence in the course of raising the child was 73%.

As expected and reported in Table 1, the milder forms of violence were more common. Slaps or spankings were mentioned by 58% of the respondents as having occurred in the previous year and by 71% of the parents as having ever taken place. During 1975 (survey year) 32% of the parents admitted pushing or shoving the referent child, while 46% stated that pushes or shoves had occurred some time in the past. Hitting with something was reported by 13% of the parents for the last year and by 20% for the duration of their raising the referent child. Throwing an object was less common—approximately 5% of the parents did this in the survey year, while fewer than 10% had ever thrown something at their referent child.

The more dangerous types of violence were the least frequent. However, extrapolating the data to the population of children 3 to 17 years of age living with both parents produces an astoundingly large number of children who were kicked, bitten, punched, beat up, threatened with a gun or a knife, or had a gun or a knife actually used on them. First, looking at the number of parents who reported each type of violence, approximately 3% of the parents reported kicking, biting, or hitting the referent child with a fist in 1975; nearly 8% stated that these acts had occurred at some point in the raising of the child. Slightly more than 1% of

Table 1: Types of Parent-to-Child Violence (N=1146)[a]

| | Occurrence in Past Year | | | | |
Incident	Once	Twice	More Than Twice	Total	Occurrence Ever
Threw Something	1.3%	1.8%	2.3%	5.4%	9.6%
Pushed/Grabbed/Shoved	4.3	9.0	18.5	31.8	46.4
Slapped or Spanked	5.2	9.4	43.6	58.2	71.0
Kicked/Bit/Hit with Fist	0.7	0.8	1.7	3.2	7.7
Hit with Something	1.0	2.6	9.8	13.4	20.0
Beat Up	0.4	0.3	0.6	1.3	4.2
Threatened with Knife/Gun	0.1	0.0	0.0	0.1	2.8
Used Knife or Gun	0.1	0.0	0.0	0.1	2.9

[a]On some items, there were a few responses omitted, but figures for all incidents represent at least 1140 families.

the respondents reported "beating up" (operationally defined as more than a single punch) the randomly selected referent child in the last year, and 4% stated that they had ever done this. One-tenth of 1%, or one in a 1,000 parents, admitted to threatening their child with a gun or a knife in 1975, while nearly three parents in 100 said they had ever threatened their child with such weapons. The same statistics were found for parents admitting actually using a gun or knife—one-tenth of a percent for the year, almost 3% ever.[3]

One can extrapolate these frequencies to estimate how many children were victims of these serious modes of violence in 1975 and how many ever faced these types of violence. There were nearly 46 million children between the ages of 3 and 17 years old who lived with both parents in 1975 (U.S. Bureau of the Census, 1975). Of these children, between 3.1 and 4.0 million have been kicked, bitten, or punched by parents at some time in their lives, while between 1.0 and 1.9 million were kicked, bitten, or punched in 1975. Between 1.4 and 2.3 million children have been "beat up" while growing up, and between 275,000 and 750,000 children 3 to 17 years old were beat up in 1975. Last, our data suggest that between 900,000 and 1.8 million American children between the ages of 3 and 17 have ever had their parents use a gun or a knife on them. Our figures do not allow for a reliable extrapolation of how many children faced parents using guns and knives in 1975, but our estimate would be something close to 46,000 children (based on an incidence of one in 1,000 children).

An examination of the data on violence used on children in 1975 indicates that violence typically represents a *pattern* of parent-child relations rather than an isolated event. Only in the case of using a gun or knife was the violent episode likely to be a one-time affair. While it is generally accepted that slaps, spankings, and shoves are frequently used techniques of child rearing, we find that even bites, kicks, punches, and using objects to hit children occur frequently in the families where they are employed.

CHILDREN AT RISK

As stated earlier, our examination of violent acts without information on the consequences of those acts prevents us from accurately estimating how many children incurred physical harm from violence during any one year. Our problem is compounded by the fact that we rely on the subject's own definition of what is meant by beating up a child. In addition, we do not know what objects were used to hit the child (a pipe or a paddle?), and we do not know how the guns or knives were deployed. Nevertheless, we felt it was important to generate an estimate of children-at-risk. We chose to compile an "at-risk" index which combined the items we felt produced the highest probability of injuring or damaging the child (kicked, bit, or hit with a fist; hit with something; beat up; threatened with a knife or a gun; used a knife or a gun). Using this index, we found that 3.6% of the parents admitted to using at least one of these modes of violence at least once in 1975. Assuming the acts we indexed have a high potential of causing harm to the intended victim, between 1.4 million and 1.9 million children were vulnerable to physical injury from violence in 1975.

A NOTE ON THE INCIDENCE DATA AND EXTRAPOLATIONS

The data on the incidence of physical violence between parents and children, and the extrapolations which produced estimates of the number of children who experienced violence and who are at risk of physical injury, ought to be considered *low estimates of violence toward children.* First, we are dealing with self-reports of violence. Although subjects who reported spanking or slapping their children may constitute an accurate estimate of incidence, the desire to give socially acceptable responses is likely to have caused many people to underreport the more serious modes of violence. If one subject in 1,000 answered that a gun or knife was used, it might be reasonable to assume that at least another one in 1,000 used these weapons and did not admit to it in the interview. Second, we interviewed only "intact" families, where both adult males and females were in the household. If, as some believe, parental violence is more common in single-parent families, then our data will underestimate the number of children experiencing potentially damaging acts from their parents. Third, we examined violence used by only one of the two parents on the referent child. Finally, our lower than expected response rate might mean that some highly violent families refused to be interviewed; if so, our incidence statistics might again be low estimates of violence toward children.

As a result of the sampling frame used and the methodological problems involved in using self-reports of violence, we see our statistics, although they may seem high to some, as being quite conservative and low estimates of the true level of violence toward children in the United States.

VIOLENCE TOWARD CHILDREN BY SEX OF PARENT

In our sample 68% of the mothers and 58% of the fathers reported at least one violent act toward their child during the survey year. Also in our sample 76% of the mothers and 71% of the fathers indicated at least one violent episode in the course of rearing their referent child. Our data on violence in the survey year indicate a small but significant difference between mothers and fathers using violence on their children. It has been frequently argued that mothers are more prone to use violence because they spend more time with their children. We hypothesize that the explanation for mothers' greater likelihood of using violence goes beyond the simple justification that they spend more time with the children. Our future analyses of the information gathered in our survey of violence in the family will examine this relationship from a number of points of view, including family power, coping ability, resources, and personality traits.

Table 2:   Parent-to-Child Violence by Sex of Parent[a]

Incident	In Past Year		Ever	
	Father	Mother	Father	Mother
Threw Something	3.6%	6.8%*	7.5%	11.3%*
Pushed/Grabbed/Shoved	29.8	33.4	35.6	39.5
Slapped or Spanked	53.3	62.5**	67.7	73.6*
Kicked/Bit/Hit with Fist	2.5	4.0	6.7	8.7
Hit with Something	9.4	16.7**	15.7	23.6**
Beat Up	0.6	1.8	4.0	4.2
Threatened with Knife/Gun	0.2	0.0	3.1	2.6
Used Knife or Gun	0.2	0.0	3.1	2.7

[a]Reports of 523 fathers and 623 mothers; figures for all incidents represent at least 520 fathers and 619 mothers.
*$x^2 \leqslant .05$.
**$x^2 \leqslant .01$.

Examining the relationship between sex of the parent and various modes of violence used on children (see Table 2), we find that, for both the survey year and the duration of the relationship, mothers are more likely to throw something at the child, slap or spank the child, or hit the child with something. There are no significant differences between mothers and fathers with respect to any of the other forms of violence. It is interesting to note that even for the most serious forms of violence (beating up; kicking, biting, punching; using guns or knives), men and women are approximately equal in their disposition to use of these modes of violence on their children. This is important because it suggests that the management of children is one of the only situations in which women are as likely as men to resort to violence.

VIOLENCE TOWARD CHILDREN BY SEX OF THE CHILD

While females are more likely to use violence in parent-child relations, male children are slightly more likely to be victims. In the survey year 66% of the sons and 61% of the daughters were struck at least once, while 76% of the male children and 71% of the females were ever hit by their parents.

Why sons are slightly more likely than daughters to be victims of parental violence is open for debate. Some might argue that boys are more difficult to raise and commit more "punishable offenses" than daughters. Another hypothesis is that our society accepts and often values boys experiencing violence because it serves to "toughen them up." The data from the 1968 National Commission on the Causes and Prevention of Violence Survey seem to bear this out in that seven in 10 people interviewed believed that it is good for a boy to have a few fist fights while he is growing up (Stark and McEvoy, 1970). Thus, experiencing violence might be considered part of the socialization process for boys and a less important "character builder" for girls (Straus, 1971).

Data on violence in the survey year (Table 3) show that the only significant difference between boys and girls was whether they were pushed, grabbed, or shoved. The other forms of violence showed no significant differences between the sexes. In the course of growing up, boys are more likely to be pushed, grabbed, shoved, spanked, or slapped.

Table 3: Parent-to-Child Violence by Sex of Child[a]

Incident	In Past Year		Ever	
	Sons	Daughters	Sons	Daughters
Threw Something	5.9%	4.4%	10.1%	8.8%
Pushed/Grabbed/Shoved	38.1	24.9**	43.9	30.7**
Slapped or Spanked	60.1	56.1	73.9	67.8*
Kicked/Bit/Hit with Fist	3.8	2.6	8.0	7.3
Hit with Something	14.9	11.2	21.5	18.1
Beat Up	1.6	0.7	4.2	4.0
Threatened with Knife/Gun	0.2	0.0	2.4	3.3
Used Knife or Gun	0.2	0.0	2.6	3.3

[a]Reports on 578 sons (responses reported for at least 574) and 547 daughters (responses for at least 545).
*$x^2 \leqslant .05$.
**$x^2 \leqslant .01$.

VIOLENCE TOWARD CHILDREN BY AGE OF THE CHILD

The literature on physical punishment and abuse of children presents various hypotheses and findings on the relationship between age and being punished or abused. A number of researchers and clinicians have proposed that the most dangerous period in a child'd life is from 3 months to 3 years of age (Fontana, 1973; Galdston, 1965; Kempe et al., 1962). Bronfenbrenner (1958) proposed that the highest rates of child abuse and battering occur among adolescents. Gil (1970) discovered that half of the confirmed cases of child abuse were children over 6 years of age, while nearly one-fifth of the confirmed reports were children in their teens.

Our survey excluded parental relations with children 3 years of age or younger, because we also studied child-to-parent violence in the interview. Thus, our data cannot be used to infer the rate of violence used on infants.

During the survey year, younger children were most likely to be victims of some form of physical force. Of children 3 and 4 years old 86% had some mode of force used on them in 1975; 82% of the children 5 to 9 had been hit; 54% of preteens and early teenage children (10 to 14 years of age) were struck; and 33% of the referent children 15 to 17 years old were hit by their parents ($x^2 - \leqslant .01$).

It appears that younger children are vulnerable to a wide range of forceful and violent acts. As shown in Table 4, preschoolers and

Table 4: Parent-to-Child Violence in Past Year by Age of Child

Incident	3-4 Years	5-9 Years	10-14 Years	15-17 Years
Threw Something	5.1%	7.0%	3.6%	5.1%
Pushed/Grabbed/Shoved	39.0	39.1	27.9	20.8[*]
Slapped or Spanked	84.1	79.9	47.9	23.0[*]
Kicked/Bit/Hit with Fist	6.2	3.2	2.2	2.5
Hit with Something	19.2	19.7	9.6	4.3[*]
Beat Up	1.1	0.9	1.1	1.7
Threatened with Knife/Gun	0.0	0.0	0.3	0.0
Used Knife or Gun	0.0	0.0	0.3	0.0
	(N=177)[a]	(N=346)[a]	(N=365)[a]	(N=236)[a]

[a]No more than three responses omitted on any category.

$^*x^2 \leqslant .01$.

children under 9 years old were more likely to be pushed, grabbed, shoved, slapped, spanked, and hit with an object. The older children seemed more vulnerable to the severest types of violence, including being beaten up and having a gun or knife used on them, although the differences are not statistically significant.

Again, there are a number of reasons why younger children are more frequent victims of parental violence. Parents may perceive difficulties in using reason to punish their younger children. A second reason might be that younger children interfere with their parents' activities more than do older children. Our future analyses of the data will focus on the factors associated with young children's susceptibility to being struck.

Discussion and Conclusions

These data on the incidence of parent-to-child violence only begin to scratch the surface of this very important topic. Our results indicate that violence toward children involves acts that go well beyond ordinary physical punishment and is an extensive and patterned phenomenon in parent-child relations. In addition, we see that mothers are the most likely users of violence, while sons and younger children are the more common victims.

A number of controversial points arise from our presentation. First, disagreement over our nominal and operational definitions of violence may lead some to disagree with our conclusion that violence is widespread in families. If someone views slaps and spankings as acceptable punishment, then they might dispute our statistics as being based on a too broadly constructed definition of violence. Although we believe there are many salient reasons for considering spankings and slaps violent, we would counter this argument by pointing to the statistics for beating up children or using a gun or a knife on a child. If a million or more children had guns or knives used on them in school, we would consider that a problem of epidemic proportions. The fact that these acts occur in the home tends to lessen concern about the impact and consequences. However, the impact and consequences are potentially dramatic, because the children are experiencing violence from those who claim love and affection for them.

A second point that will be raised about our findings is the question of bias and whether our respondents actually told the truth. We have spent seven years developing and testing the instruments used in this study. However, we do not know the actual validity of our findings or whether our subjects "told the truth." The major bias in this study of family violence is likely to be one of underreporting. We doubt that many subjects will report beating up their children or using a gun or a knife on them when they did not. Thus, our statistics are probably underestimates of the true level of parent-child violence in the United States. If one considers the possibility that, for every subject who admitted using a knife or a gun, an additional subject used these weapons but did not admit it, then our estimates of risk could be doubled to produce a true estimate of risk of physical violence.

Another issue that will be pursued after examining our data, and an issue we will pursue in later analyses, is the fact that people actually admitted using severe and dangerous forms of physical violence. Our tentative explanation of this is that many of our subjects did not consider kicking, biting, punching, beating up, shooting, or stabbing their children deviant. In other words, they may have admitted to these acts because they felt they were acceptable or tolerable ways of bringing up children. Thus, it may be that one major factor contributing to the high level of parent-child violence we have found is the normative acceptability of hitting one's children.

Despite the methodological problems, this is the first survey of parent-to-child violence based on a true cross-section of American families. Thus, the data presented here probably come closer to describing the real situation of violence toward children in America than anything available until now.

NOTES

1. The completion rate for the entire sample was 65%, varying from a low of 60% in metropolitan areas to a high of 72.3% in other areas.

2. Copies of the scale used, containing questionnaire items and response categories, are available from the author on request.

3. We do not know exactly what is meant by *using* a gun or knife. It could mean a parent threw a knife at the child, or it could mean attempting to stab or actually stabbing the child; a gun could have been fired without the child being wounded. However, the fact is that these parents admit using the weapon, not just threatening its use.

Part II

MARITAL VIOLENCE

Introduction

MARITAL VIOLENCE

As with violence toward children, there is no evidence which can be drawn on to estimate the incidence of marital violence in the United States and around the world over the last few hundred years. However, the historical and legal data which are available demonstrate that domestic violence has not been confined to parent-child relationships. Del Martin (1976) and Terry Davidson (1978) reviewed the history of wife abuse and report that wives have been raped, choked, stabbed, shot, beaten, had their jaws broken and have been struck with whips, pokers, bats and bicycle chains for as long as we have records of family life.

Legal precedents sanctioned, to a degree, the right of a husband to use violence on his wife. The classic "rule of thumb" gave legal justification to common law which allowed a husband to strike his wife with a switch, provided the stick was no larger than his thumb.

Despite a long standing social and legal attitude which favored the use of violence between partners, it was not until the 1970s that scientific, legal, and public attention was directed towards the problem of "wife battering." Since 1975, there has been increased attention to the violence used by wives. Cases such as that of

Francine Hughes, a Michigan housewife who poured gasoline under the bed of her sleeping husband and ignited him and the bed have generated discussions of the so-called problem of "battered husbands."

Our study of family violence which produced the statistical estimates of the extent of child abuse reported in the previous section also measured the extent of violence between spouses. We found that one out of every six couples in the United States engage in at least one incident of violence each year (Straus, Gelles, and Steinmetz, 1979). Over the course of a marriage the chances are greater than one in four (28%) that a couple will come to blows.

As with violence towards children, the "milder" forms of violence are the most common types of interspousal assaults. Throwing an object, slapping, spanking, pushing and grabbing are the most likely types of violence to occur.

Using the same kind of index we used to measure child abuse, we measured the level of spouse abuse. Nearly four in 100 women are physically abused by their husbands each year (3.8%). The figure for husbands is higher—4.6% are victims of severe physical violence. It would appear, if one uses just these figures, that husband beating is more common than wife beating. We examine this hypothesis in greater detail in the last essay in this section, "The Truth About Husband Abuse."

The statistics on marital violence projected for the 47 million marriages in the United States indicate that no fewer than 2 million women are victims of severe physical violence each year. As we mentioned at the start of this section, marital violence is not a new thing and there is no evidence which could allow us to conclude that the rates we report for wife abuse are higher or lower than the rates 10, 20, or even 100 years ago.

Despite the fact that the marriage license has always been a hitting license (Straus, 1974b) and despite the fact that the incidence of spouse beating, if found in any other institution or social group would be called an epidemic, the majority of the public still does not consider the problem of spouse battering as serious as the problem of battered children. In large part, this is due to the fact that children (especially young children and infants) are viewed as helpless and innocent victims of their parents' rage. Battered wives, on the other hand, are frequently viewed with suspicion and often contempt. Discussion of specific cases of wife battering often leads to inevitable comments, "but what did *she* do to deserve it?" or "don't some women really like the violence?" Women who attempt to leave violent husbands are chastised for not trying hard enough to keep their marriages together; and, women who stay with their violent husbands, hoping that they will change, are labeled "masochists."

The situation for spouses who want help and assistance is frustrating and often futile. While all 50 states have child abuse laws which include definitions of abuse and procedures for reporting and treating cases, few states have domestic violence laws (one state which has such a law is Massachusetts). While every state in the country provides an agency to intervene on the behalf of and protect battered children, the number of shelters for battered spouses in the country are few (less than 100), and they are often meagerly funded by private contributions.

The first three essays in this section on marital violence consider the situation of the woman victim. In "Abused Wives: Why Do They Stay?" we explode the myth that women who remain with assaultive husbands are masochistic. In "Violence and Pregnancy: A Note on the Extent of the Problem and Needed Services" we identify one situation in family life which dramatically increases the risk of domestic violence. "Power, Sex, and Violence: The Case of Marital Rape" uncovers a topic which few people have ever considered—domestic sexual assault. Finally, "The Truth About Husband Abuse" goes beyond an analysis of whether husbands are likely to be abused by their wives and discusses the general problem of spouse abuse and what steps could be taken to ameliorate the problem.

Chapter 5

ABUSED WIVES: WHY DO THEY STAY?

Why would a woman who has been physically abused by her husband remain with him? This question is one of the most frequently asked by both professionals and the lay public in the course of discussions of family violence, and one of the more difficult to adequately answer. The question itself derives from the elementary assumption that any reasonable individual, having been beaten and battered by another person, would avoid being victimized again (or at least avoid the attacker). Unfortunately, the answer to why women remain with their abusive husbands is not nearly as simple as the assumption that underlies the question. In the first place, the decision to either stay with an assaultive spouse or to seek intervention or dissolution of a marriage is not related solely to the extent or severity of the physical assault. Some spouses will suffer repeated severe beatings or even stabbings without so much as calling a neighbor, while others call the police after a coercive gesture from their husbands. Second, the assumption that the victim would flee from a conjugal attacker overlooks

From Richard J. Gelles, "Abused Wives: Why Do They Stay?" *Journal of Marriage and the Family,* 1976, 38 (November): 659-668.

the complex subjective meaning of intrafamilial violence, the nature of commitment and entrapment to the family as a social group, and the external constraint which limits a woman's ability to seek outside help. As has been reported elsewhere (Parnas, 1967; Gelles, 1974; Straus, 1974b, 1976), violence between spouses is often viewed as normative and, in fact, mandated in family relations. Wives have reported that they believe that it is acceptable for a husband to beat his wife "every once in a while" (Parnas, 1967: 952; Gelles, 1974: 59-61).

This essay attempts to provide an answer to the question of why victims of conjugal violence stay with their husbands by focusing on various aspects of the family and family experience which distinguish between women who seek intervention or disso- lution of a marriage as a response to violence and those women who suffer repeated beatings without seeking outside interven- tion.[1] We shall specifically analyze how previous experience with family violence affects the decision to seek intervention, and how the extent of violence, educational status, occupational status, number of children, and age of oldest child influence the wife's actions in responding to assaults from her husband. Finally, we shall discuss how external constraints lessen the likelihood of a woman seeking intervention in conjugal assaults.

Victims of Family Violence

Although no one has systematically attempted to answer the question of why an abused wife would stay with her husband, there has been some attention focused on women who attempt to seek intervention after being beaten by their husbands. Snell, Rosenwald, and Robey (1964) examined 12 clinical cases to determine why a wife takes her abusive husband to court. They begin by stating that the question answers itself (because he beats her!), but they go on to explain that the decision to seek legal assistance is the result of a change in the wife's behavior, not the husband's, because many wives report a history of marital violence when they did not seek assistance.

Truninger (1971) found that women attempt to dissolve a violent marriage only after a history of conflict and reconciliation. According to this analysis, a wife makes a decision to obtain a divorce from her abusive husband when she can no longer believe her husband's promises of no more violence nor forgive past episodes of violence. Truninger postulates that some of the reasons women *do not* break off relationships with abusive husbands are that: (1) they have negative self-concepts; (2) they believe their husbands will reform; (3) economic hardship; (4) they have children who need a father's economic support; (5) they doubt they can get along alone; (6) they believe divorcees are stigmatized; and (7) it is difficult for women with children to get work. Although this analysis attempts to explain why women remain with abusive husbands, the list does not specify which factors are the most salient in the wife's decision to either stay or seek help.

There are a number of other factors which help explain the wife's decision to stay or get help in cases of violence. Straus (1973) states that self-concept and role expectations of others often influence what is considered to be an intolerable level of violence by family members. Scanzoni's (1972) exchange model of family relations postulates that the ratio of rewards to punishments is defined subjectively by spouses and is the determining factor in deciding whether to stay married or not. The decision of whether or not to seek intervention or dissolution of a marriage may be partly based on the subjective definitions attached to the violence (punishment) and partly on the ratio of this punishment to other marital rewards (security, companionship, and the like).

Additional research on violence between husbands and wives suggests that severity of violence has an influence on the wife's actions (see O'Brien, 1971 and Levinger, 1966 for discussion of petitioners for divorce and their experience with violence). Research on victims of violence sheds little additional light on the actions of abused wives (Straus, 1976).[2]

Methodology

Data for this study were derived from interviews with members of 80 families. An unstructured informal interview procedure was employed to facilitate data collection on the sensitive topic of intrafamilial violence. For this study 20 families suspected of using violence were chosen from the files of a private social service agency. Another 20 families were selected by examining a police "blotter" to locate families in which the police had been summoned to break up violent disputes. An additional 40 families were interviewed by selecting one neighboring family for each "agency" or "police" family.[3]

The interviews were carried out in two cities in New Hampshire. The sampling procedure employed enhanced the likelihood of locating families in which violence had occurred, but it also meant that this sample was not representative of any larger populations.

Major limitations of this study are that it is exploratory in nature, the sample is small, and the representativeness of the sample is unknown. The small sample, the unknown representativeness, and the possible biases that enter into the study as a result of the sampling procedure all impinge on the generalizability of the findings presented in this essay.

There are, however, strengths in the study which tend to offset the limitations of sample design and sample size. First, this is a unique study. The area of spousal violence has long suffered from selective inattention (Dexter, 1958) on the part of both society and the research community. While some data has been gathered on the topic of family violence, most of the studies focus on one type of population—either petitioners for divorce (O'Brien, 1971; Levinger, 1966), patients of psychiatrists (Snell, Rosenwald, and Robey, 1964), or college students (Straus, 1974b; Steinmetz, 1974). This study is one of the few which examines not only those in special circumstances (agency clients or those calling police), but also an equal number of families who had no contact with agencies of social service or control.[4] While the sample is obviously not representative, it is one of the closest yet to a study of violence in a cross-section of families.

A second strength of the methodology is that it yielded a population without a working-class, lower-class, or middle-class bias. The sample ranged from families at the lowest regions of socioeconomic status, to middle-class families in which one or both spouses had graduated from college and had a combined family income exceeding $25,000. (For a complete discussion of the social characteristics of the respondents and their families, see Gelles, 1974: 205-215.)

Although the methodology was not designed specifically to address the issue posed in this essay it turned out to be particularly well suited for the proposed analysis. The sampling technique yielded wives who called the police, wives who were clients of a social service agency, and wives who had never sought any outside intervention.

The interviews with the 80 family members yielded 41 women who had been physically struck by their husbands during their marriage. Of these, nine women had been divorced or separated from their husbands; 13 had called on the police and were still married; eight sought counseling from a private social service agency (because of violence and other family problems); and 11 had sought no outside intervention.

Findings

We derived some ideas and predictions concerning factors which distinguished between beaten wives who obtained outside intervention and those who did not attempt to bring in outside resources or file for a divorce. These ideas are based on the interviews with the 41 members of violent families and on previous research on family violence. We utilized both quantitative and qualitative data obtained from the interviews to assess the effect of: (1) severity and frequency of violence; (2) experience and exposure to violence in one's family of orientation; (3) education and occupation of the wife, number of children, and age of oldest child; and (4) external constraint on the actions of the victimized wife.

SEVERITY AND FREQUENCY OF VIOLENCE

Common sense suggests that if violence is severe enough or frequent enough, a wife will eventually attempt to either flee from her abusive husband or to bring in some mediator to protect her from violence.

In order to analyze whether severity of violence influenced the reactions of the wife, we constructed a 10-point scale of violence severity (0=no violence; 1=pushed or shoved; 2=threw object; 3=slapped or bit; 4=punched or kicked; 5=pushed down; 6=hit with hard object; 7=choked; 8=stabbed; 9=shot).[5] This scale measured the most severe violence the wife had ever experienced as a victim.

Table 1 indicates that the more severe the violence, the more likely the wife is to seek outside assistance. An examination of wives' reactions to particular instances of violence reveals even more about the impact of violence severity on the actions of abused wives. Of the eight women who were either shot at (one), choked (six), or hit with a hard object (one), five had obtained divorces, two had called the police, and one had sought counseling from a social service agency. At the other extreme, of the nine women who had been pushed or shoved (eight), or had objects thrown at them (one), one had gotten a divorce, one had called the police, and seven had sought no assistance at all.

How frequently a wife is hit also influences her decision whether to remain with her husband, call the police, go to a social worker, or seek dissolution of the marriage. Only 42% of the women who had been struck once in the marriage had sought some type of intervention, while 100% of the women who had been hit at least once in a month and 83% of the women who had been struck at least once a week had either obtained a divorce or separation, called the police, or went to a social service agency. Frequency of violence is also related to what type of intervention a wife seeks. Women hit weekly to daily are most likely to call the police, while women hit less often (at least once a month) are more inclined to get a divorce or legal separation.

There are a number of plausible explanations as to why frequency of violence influences mode of intervention. Perhaps the more frequent the violence, the more a wife wants immediate protection, whereas victims of monthly violence gradually see less value in staying married to a husband who explodes occasionally.

Table 1: Violence Severity by Intervention Mode

Intervention	Mean Violence Severity
No Intervention	2.1
Divorced or Separated	5.1
Called Police	4.0
Went to Agency	4.6
Total for all who sought intervention	4.6

F=5.2 Statistically significant at the .01 level.

A possible explanation of the findings might be that women who were divorced or separated were ashamed to admit they tolerated violence as long as they did (for fear of being labeled "sadomasochists"). Also, it may be that victims of frequent violence are afraid of seeking a temporary or permanent separation. Victims of weekly violence may be terrorized by their violent husbands and view police intervention as more tolerable to their husbands than a divorce or separation. Finally, women who are struck frequently might feel that a separation or divorce might produce a radical and possibly lethal reaction from an already violent husband.

EXPERIENCE WITH AND EXPOSURE TO VIOLENCE AS A CHILD

Studies of murderers (Gillen, 1946; Guttmacher, 1960; Leon, 1969; Palmer, 1962; Tanay, 1969), child abusers (Bakan, 1971; Gelles, 1973; Gil, 1971; Kempe et al., 1962; Steele and Pollock, 1974), and violent spouses (Gelles, 1974; Owens and Straus, 1975) support the assumption that the more individuals are exposed to violence as children (both as observers and victims), the more they are violent as adults. The explanation offered for this relationship is that the experience with violence as a victim and observer teaches the individual how to be violent and also to approve of the use of violence. In other words, exposure to violence provides a "role model" for violence (Singer, 1971). If experience with violence can provide a role model for the offender, then perhaps it can also provide a role model for the victim.

Women who observed spousal violence in their family of orientation were more likely to be victims of conjugal violence in their family of procreation. Of the 54 women who never saw their parents fight physically, 46% were victims of spousal violence, while 66% of the 12 women who observed their parents exchange blows were later victims of violent attacks. In addition, the more frequently a woman was struck by her parents, the more likely she was to grow up and be struck by her husband.[6]

There are two interrelated reasons why women who were exposed to or were victims of intrafamilial violence would be prone to be the victims of family violence as adults. It is possible that the more experience with violence a woman has, the more she is inclined to approve of the use of violence in the family. She may grow up with the expectation that husbands are "supposed" to hit wives, and this role expectation may in turn become the motivator for her husband to use violence on her. Another explanation of these findings integrates the subculture theory of violence (Wolfgang and Ferracuti, 1967) with the homogamy theory of mate selection (Centers, 1949; Ecklund, 1968; Hollingshead, 1950). Thus, it could be argued that women who grew up in surroundings which included and approved of family violence, are more likely to marry a person who is prone to use violence.

Given the fact that being a victim of violence as a child or seeing one's parents physically fight makes a woman more vulnerable to becoming the victim of conjugal violence, does exposure and experience with violence as a child affect *the actions* of a beaten wife? There are two alternative predictions that could be made. First, the less a woman experienced violence in her family of orientation, the more likely she is to view intrafamilial violence as deviant, and thus, the more she is willing to seek intervention or a divorce when hit by her husband. On the other hand, exposure to violence may provide a role model for the woman as to what to do when attacked. Thus, the *more* violence she was exposed to, the more she will know about how to get outside help, and the more she will seek this help.

Table 2: Intervention Mode by Wife's Experience with Violence as a Child[7]

| | Type of Intervention | | | |
	Divorced or Separated	Called Police	Went to Agency	Total Seeking Intervention
Type of Experience as Child				
A. *Parents Violent to Respondent*				
None (N=3)	33%	0%	66%	100%
Infrequent* (N=13)	23%	38%	15%	76%
Frequent+ (N=17)	24%	35%	18%	77%
B. *Parents Violent to Each Other*				
None observed (N=25)	28%	28%	20%	76%
Observed (N=8)	63%	13%	13%	89%

*less than 6 times a year
+from monthly to daily

Being a victim of parental violence and frequency of victimization appear to have no bearing on the beaten wife's decision whether or not to seek outside intervention[7] (Table 2). Those women who observed their parents engaged in physical fights were slightly more likely to obtain outside intervention after being hit by their husbands. For those women who did see their parents engage in conjugal violence, the predominant mode of intervention in their own family of procreation was a divorce or separation. There is no predominant mode of intervention chosen by those women who did not witness violence in their families of orientation.

Thus, neither of the alternative predictions is strongly supported by the data on experience and exposure to violence. There is the suggestion that exposure to conjugal violence makes women *less tolerant* of family violence and more desirous of ending a violent marriage. Along these lines, some of the women we interviewed stated that after they saw their parents fight they vowed that they would never stand for their own husbands hitting them. However, the data do not support the claim that this position is widespread among wives who witnessed violence as they grew up.

EDUCATION, OCCUPATION, NUMBER OF CHILDREN, AGE OF CHILDREN

Truninger (1971) has proposed that the stronger the commitment to marriage, the less a wife will seek legal action against a violent husband. We have modified this hypothesis by proposing that the fewer resources a wife has in a marriage, the fewer alternatives she has in her marriage; and the more "entrapped" she is in the marriage, the more reluctant she will be to seek outside intervention. Thus, we hypothesize that unemployed wives with low education will not do anything when beaten. It is difficult to predict what influence number of children and age of children have on the actions of the wife. Snell, Rosenwald and Robey (1964) state that the presence of an older child motivates women to take their husbands to court.

Looking at the relationship between each variable and intervention, we see that the variable which best distinguishes wives who obtain assistance from those who remain with their husbands is holding a job. While only 25% of those wives who sought no help

Table 3:   Education, Occupation, Number of Children, Age of Oldest Child
           by Intervention Mode

	Mean Education	Percent Completed High School	Percent Employed	Mean Number of Children	Mean Age of Oldest Child
No Intervention (N=11)	11.9	63%	25%	2.5	9.3
Divorced or Separated (N=9)	11.7	66%	44%*	3.3	9.3
Called Police (N=13)	11.0	69%	38%	3.0	13.0
Went to Agency (N=8)	11.1	62%	75%	2.6	13.7
All Intervention	11.3	67%	50%	3.0	12.0

*For those wives who are divorced or separated, some may have found employment *after* the divorce or separation. The data did not allow us to determine *when* the wife found employment.

worked, 50% of the wives who called the police, went to a social service agency, or were separated or divorced from their husbands held jobs. This confirms our hypothesis that the more resources a wife has, the more she is able to support herself and her children, the more she will have a low threshold of violence and call outside agents or agencies to help her. Thus, the less dependent a wife is on her husband, the more likely she is to call for help in instances of violence. In addition to this resource dimension, wives reported that holding a job gave them a view of another world or culture. This new perspective made their own family problems seem less normal and more serious than they had felt when they were at home. This point is illustrated in the following excerpt from one of our interviews with a woman who was the client of a social service agency and who had been beaten by her husband when they were first married:

> Until I started being out in the public, to realize what was going on around me, I was so darned stupid and ignorant. I didn't know how the other half of the world lived. And when I started being a waitress I used to love to sit there—when I wasn't busy—and watch the people—the mother and the father with their children—and see how they acted. And I started to feel like I was cheated . . . and it started to trouble me and I started to envy those people. So I said, "you know . . . am I supposed to live the way I'm living?"

Women who called the police or went to an agency often had teenage children. The data confirm the Snell, Rosenwald, and Robey (1964) finding that women who brought their husbands to court had teenage children. In some of our interviews, wives reported that they started calling the police when their son or daughter was old enough to get embroiled in the physical conflicts. In these cases, the wives wanted to help to protect their children rather than themselves.

Neither education (measured by mean years of school completed and completed high school) nor number of children distinguishes between abused women seeking help and those staying with their husbands.

COMBINED EFFECTS OF VARIABLES ON INTERVENTION

Up to this point we have examined the effects of the variables which we believed would be likely determinants of whether or not a wife sought intervention. This analysis, however, does not allow us to assess the effects of all these variables in explaining whether or not a wife would seek outside help in cases of conjugal violence. In order to examine the impact of all the variables together, we employed a step-wise multiple regression procedure which allowed us to see what proportion of the variance of intervention or particular intervention modalities is explained by combinations of the independent variables.[8]

Intervention. Table 4 reveals that the best predictor of whether or not a wife seeks intervention is violence severity in her family of procreation. Thus, women who seek intervention are strongly influenced by the level of violence in their family. The five variables entered into the regression analysis explain 32% of the variance in seeking intervention or not.

Divorced or Separated. The best predictor of whether or not a wife obtains a divorce or separation is the level of violence in her family of procreation. The combined effect of all the variables entered into the equation is the explanation of 14% of the variance in the dependent variable; however, the multiple Rs are not statistically significant at the .05 level.

Called Police. We are able to explain 11% of the variance in this variable, but again, multiple Rs are not statistically significant at the .05 level. Unlike separation or divorce, in which cases severity

Table 4:   Step-wise Regression of Independent Variables and Intervention
           and Intervention Modalities

	Mulitple R	R^2	Beta
A. Regression of Intervention on:			
Violence Severity	.434#	.189	.365
Completed High School	.488#	.238	.331
Parental Violence to Respondent	.530#	.280	-.260
Frequency of Violence	.559#	.312	.221
Wife's Occupational Status*	.570#	.324	-.136
B. Regression of Divorced or Separated on:			
Violence Severity	.281	.080	.211
Wife's Education	.314	.099	.298
Frequency of Violence	.324	.105	.154
Completed High School	.340	.115	-.136
Wife's Occupational Status*	.347	.120	.089
Violence Between Parents	.352	.124	-.027
Number of Children	.355	.126	.261
Age of Oldest Child	.373	.140	.231
C. Regression of Called Police on:			
Wife's Occupational Status*	.195	.038	-.231
Completed High School	.256	.065	.423
Wife's Education	.314	.099	-.245
Parental Violence to Respondent	.319	.101	-.016
Age of Oldest Child	.324	.105	-.233
Number of Children	.340	.115	.233
D. Regression of Went to Agency on:			
Parental Violence to Respondent	.326+	.106	-.191
Age of Oldest Child	.350	.122	.480
Number of Children	.425+	.180	-.496
Violence Severity	.442	.196	.114

#statistically significant at the .01 level
+statistically significant at the .05 level
*Occupational Status measured using Bureau of Census status score (see Robinson,
Athanasiou, and Head, 1969:357).

and extent of violence in her family of procreation played major
roles in the wife's actions, the calling of police is associated with
the wife's occupational status and her education. Women with less
occupational status and lower education are likely to call the
police for help. This finding is consistent with the popular assumption that the poor man's social worker is the police officer.

Went to Agency. The best predictor of going to a social service
agency is how much violence the wife experienced as a child. The
less violence, the more likely she is to seek a social worker's help.

In contrast to the previous dependent variables, age and number of children play a greater part in influencing a wife's decision to go to a social service agency. Almost 20% of the variance in seeking agency assistance is explained by the four variables included in the regression.

EXTERNAL CONSTRAINT

The fact that a woman would call the police or seek agency assistance after repeated incidents of conjugal violence does not necessarily mean that she will call the police again or continue going to an agency. One fact remained quite clear at the end of the 80 interviews: most agencies and most legal organizations are quite unprepared and unable to provide meaningful assistance to women who have been beaten by their husbands. With minor exceptions, such as the work done by Bard and his colleagues (1969; 1969; 1971), little formal training has been given to police in how to intercede in conjugal disputes. Truninger (1971) reports that the courts are often mired in mythology about family violence (e.g., "violence fulfills the masochistic need of women victims") and consequently the justice system is ineffective in dealing with marital violence. Field and Field (1973: 225) echo these sentiments and state that unless the victim dies, the chances that the court system will deal seriously with the offender are slight. Women who are abused by their husbands must suffer grave injury in order to press legal charges. The California Penal Code states that a wife must be more injured than commonly allowed for battery to press charges against her husband (Calvert, 1974: 89). As Field and Field (1973) state, there is an official acceptance of violence between "consenting" adults and the belief that this violence is a private affair. This attitude, held by police, the courts, and the citizenry, constrains many wives from either seeking initial help, or once obtaining help, continuing to use it.

Although social work agencies are not as "indifferent" about marital violence as the courts and police are (Field and Field, 1973: 236), they are often unable to provide realistic answers for victims of violence because of the rather limited amount of knowledge in this area. The data on marital violence are so scanty that few policy or intervention strategies have been worked out for the use of social workers. Without a good knowledge of the causes and patterns of marital violence, many social workers have had to rely on stop-gap measures which never address the real problem of marital violence.

A final source of external constraint is the wife's fear that the myth of her peaceful family life will be exploded. Many women we spoke to would never think of calling the police, going to a social work agency, or filing for a divorce because those actions would rupture the carefully nurtured myth of their fine family life. One woman, who had been struck often and hard over a 30-year marriage said she would never call the police because she was afraid it would appear in the papers. Truninger (1971: 264) supports these findings by stating that part of the reason why the courts are ineffective in dealing with marital violence is the strong social pressure on individuals to keep marital altercations private.

In summary, even if a woman wants to get help and protection from her husband, she all too frequently finds out that the agents and agencies she calls are ineffective or incapable of providing real assistance. During the course of the interviews, many wives who had sought intervention complained about the futility of such actions. One woman in particular had sought agency help, called the police, and finally filed for a divorce. However, none of these actions actually protected her, and her estranged husband almost strangled her one weekend morning.

The deficiencies of these external agencies and the pressure to cover up family altercations are two powerful forces which keep women with their abusive husbands.

Conclusion

The purpose of this essay has been to address the important question of why victims of conjugal violence stay with their husbands. Our analysis of the variables which affect the decision to either stay with an abusive husband or to seek intervention, uncovered three major factors which influence the actions of abused women. First, the less severe and the less frequent the violence, the more a woman will remain with her spouse and not seek outside aid. This finding is almost self-evident in that it posits that women seek intervention when they are severely abused. However, the problem is more complex, because severity and frequency of violence explain only part of the variance in abused wives' behavior. A second factor is how much violence a wife experiences as a child. The more she was struck by her parents, the more inclined she is to stay with her abusive husband. It appears that victimization as a child raises the wife's tolerance for violence as an adult. Finally, educational and occupational factors are associated with staying with an abusive husband. Wives who do not seek intervention are less likely to have completed high school and more likely to be unemployed. We conclude that the fewer resources a woman has, the less power she has, and the more entrapped she is in her marriage, the more she suffers at the hands of her husband without calling for help outside the family.

Another factor which appears to influence the actions of a wife is external constraint in the form of police, agency, and court lack of understanding about marital violence.

Although we have presented some factors which partly explain why abused wives remain with their husbands, we have not provided a complete answer to the question this essay raises. The reason for this is that the factors influencing the reactions of an abused wife are tremendously complex. It is not simply how hard or how often a wife is hit, nor is it how much education or income she has. The decision of whether or not to seek intervention is the result of a complex interrelationship of factors, some of which have been identified in this essay.

Although we have provided tentative answers to the central question of this essay, a main underlying issue of this topic has not been addressed. Even though more than 75% of the women who had been struck had tried to get outside help, the end result of this intervention was not totally satisfactory. The outlook for women who are physically beaten and injured by their husbands is not good. For those who have few resources, no job, and no idea of how to get help, the picture is grim. But even the women who have the resources and desire to seek outside help often find this help of little benefit.

NOTES

1. While we would have liked to answer the same question for men who were struck by their wives, we interviewed too few men who had been hit by their wives to conduct any meaningful data analysis.

2. Because we are focusing on the reactions of victims of intrafamilial violence, we had hoped that some insight could be gained from the literature on "victimology." "Victimology" is defined by its proponents (see Drapkin and Viano, 1974, Hentig, 1948, and Schafer, 1968) as the scientific study of the criminal-victim relationship. However, the current work on these relationships does not focus specifically on factors which lead victims to sever relationships with offenders or to obtain outside intervention. Because victimologists' analyses of marital violence are typically limited to cases of homicide (see Wolfgang, 1957), there are few insights to be gained for the purposes of this essay from the study of the literature on the criminal-victim relationship.

3. For a complete discussion of the methodology, including an evaluation of the sampling procedure and instrument see Gelles, 1974: 36-43.

4. Another study which examines a cross section of families is Steinmetz (1975) multimethod examination of 57 families randomly selected from New Castle County, Delaware. The sample size is small, but it is representative, if only of one county in Delaware.

5. For the purposes of this analysis, we viewed each higher point on the scale as more severe than the previous category of violence. In addition, we treated the scale as interval data in order to conduct a one-way Analysis of Variance. The scale was treated as an interval measure because this was the only possible way to assess the impact of violence severity on the wives.

6. Many individuals may find it difficult to label the use of physical force on children as violence. This is because there are many powerful pro-use-of-physical-force-on-children norms in our society (Straus, 1976). If one defines violence as an act with the intent of physically injuring the victim, then physically punishing a child is violent. Note, a complete tabular presentation of these data is available from the author.

7. Although this study deals with 41 families where the wife was a victim of violence, Table 2 presents only 33 wives who were victims of violence. The smaller number of wives occurs because in some of the 41 families we interviewed the husband and have no data on the wife's experience with violence. Some other women reported that they were brought up in foster homes or by one parent, and thus we have no "exposure to violence data" for these women.

8. In order to conduct this analysis the dependent variables (Intervention, Divorce or Separated, Called Police, and Went to an Agency) were transformed into "dummy" variables. Each variable was treated as a dichotomy (e.g., "Sought Intervention" or "Did Not Seek Intervention"). Certain ordinal variables (violence severity, completed high school, violence frequency, parental violence to respondent, and violence between parents) are treated as interval measures.

Chapter 6

VIOLENCE AND PREGNANCY: A NOTE ON THE
EXTENT OF THE PROBLEM AND NEEDED SERVICES

In a society which publicly views the birth of a child as a "blessed" event, one does not ordinarily think of pregnancy and interpersonal violence as events which coincide in family life. However, a startling discovery in a study on violence between husbands and wives (Gelles, 1974) was that a number of wives stated that they were physically attacked while they were pregnant. Although there has been research on parenthood as crisis (Le Masters, 1957, Dyer, 1963, Hobbs, 1965), few students of family relations have been aware of the crisis of pregnancy and that this often leads to physical violence. This essay examines the phenomenon of violence toward pregnant wives and posits that it is possible that violence in pregnancy is common enough to be considered an important empirical issue by researchers and practitioners in the field of family relations.

From Richard J. Gelles, "Violence and Pregnancy: A Note on the Extent of the Problem and Needed Services," *Family Coordinator*, 1975, 24 (January): 81-86.

During the conduct of our first study of family violence it became evident that many of the wives who were physically struck by their husbands were hit during the term of their pregnancy. Members of 80 families were interviewed. In more than half of these families (55%) at least one incident of conjugal violence was discussed. In 10 of these 44 families respondents discussed incidents of violence occurring while the wife was pregnant (Gelles, 1974).

Because the sample interviewed was nonrepresentative, it is impossible to generalize the findings beyond these 80 families. However, the fact that violence occurred during pregnancy in almost one-quarter of the families reporting violence, indicates that this could be a phenomenon of widespread occurrence. Other sources of information support the notion that physical violence and pregnancy are more highly associated than is commonly realized. For instance, many newspaper accounts of intrafamilial violence and homicide note that the wife/victim, was pregnant at the time of the attack. For example:

A 20-year-old youth accused of strangling his pregnant wife hanged himself last night from a knotted bedsheet in his cell at Clinton County jail [New York Sunday Times, August 26, 1973].

Reports from Britain indicate that beatings during pregnancy are relatively common (Newsweek, 1973: 39; Mindout, 1974).

In addition to these sources of information, evidence comes from a third and more surprising source, contemporary American fiction. Steinmetz and Straus (1974) in an anthology of articles dealing with family violence note that they were unable to locate a single passage in American fiction where a husband or a wife beat each other (with the exception of cases where the protagonist is already labeled a deviant from some other activity—i.e., murderer or criminal, or where the participants are foreign). However, there are three cases in American fiction where violence between spouses is portrayed and the beaten wife is pregnant during the attack. In Puzo's *The Godfather* (1969), the Don's daughter is beaten by her husband while she is pregnant; Rhette Butler throws Scarlette down the stairs while she is pregnant in *Gone With The Wind* (Mitchell, 1936); and in Mary MacCarthy's *The Group,* a pregnant wife is also assaulted by her husband (1963).

Clearly, the exact extent of violence during pregnancy is still an empirical question; however, the examples cited support the tentative hypothesis that violence and pregnancy are somehow associated, such that an important aspect of research and examinations of intrafamily violence ought to focus on violence which occurs during a wife's term of pregnancy.

Why Violence During Pregnancy

The interviews with women who were beaten during their pregnancy give some insight into the causes behind the association between being pregnant and being beaten by one's husband. In addition, research on family transitions and on violence contribute other possible answers to this question. We propose that there are five major factors which contribute to pregnant wives being assaulted by their husbands: (1) sexual frustration, (2) family transition, stress, and strain, (3) biochemical changes in the wife, (4) prenatal child abuse, and (5) defenselessness of the wife.

SEXUAL FRUSTRATION

A number of social workers whom we spoke to in connection with the finding on violence during pregnancy commented that it might well be caused by the sexual frustration which arises during pregnancy. Although doctors now inform prospective parents that there is only a brief period during which couples should abstain from sexual intercourse, pregnancy in many families is taken as the sign that sexual relations must cease. The reasons behind this abstinence range from superstition (a husband was afraid the baby would bite him, Congdon, 1970), to the husband's lack of interest in his physically changing wife. One woman interviewed commented that she was hit during her pregnancy and that her husband's sexual habits at this time were "peculiar":

Interviewer: Did he ever hit you when you were pregnant?
Mrs. (10): Oh yes, this was his pastime. Plus, he's uh, his sex life—I don't know what you would call it a homosexual or what. We would have sex relations and he would have a jar of vaseline. If things weren't going right he would go into the bathroom and masturbate.

TRANSITION AND STRESS

Rossi (1968) discussed at length the transition to parenthood and its implications for role relations and role changes in the family. She labels the onset of the pregnancy as the end of the honeymoon stage of the marriage. For many families the transition to parenthood and the resulting effect on family structure create a number of stresses and strains for the husband and wife as the due date approaches.

When a man and woman marry because the woman is pregnant the honeymoon stage ends rather rapidly—if it ever existed. Husbands who marry pregnant wives may feel increasing stress as the baby approaches (or as the wife swells). Mrs. (70), who was beaten often during her pregnancy, discusses the tremendous strain her husband was under because he was forced into the marriage:

> Mrs. (70):   Our problem was getting married and having a baby so fast . . . that produced a great strain . . . I wasn't ready. I had the baby six months after we were married.

A similar problem of a too rapid transition to parenthood occurs if the baby is conceived shortly after the couple is married.

> Mrs. (59):   I think because neither of us were ready to have any children—and I got pregnant about three months after I was married. He never accepted it really. He loved to ski and hike. We had a place we could go to weekends and he didn't want to stop doing anything—and if I couldn't go he would go without me.

In Mrs. (59)'s marriage, as in marriages of other women we talked to, the pregnancy caused a change in the family routine. Often the husband did not want to change his routine of work and leisure. This led to conflict, arguments, and in some instances violence.

It is obvious that these women are not the only ones who suffer from the stress and strain of being pregnant, nor are these the only families for whom pregnancy brings about a rapid transition and change in family role relations. The crucial point in bringing about violence was that the stress of pregnancy was added on to an already high level of structural stress in these families. Half of the 10 families had less than a $5,000 a year income in 1972. Two husbands were unemployed and five more were seasonally employed (painters, construction work). In addition, only one husband had a high school diploma. So there is evidence that these families were already under economic stress when the pregnancy occurred. The role changes and potential new mouth to feed add to the stress level.

BIOCHEMICAL CHANGES IN THE WIFE

Another source of stress during this transitional period is the biochemical changes which are occurring in the wife. Women often describe the onset of pregnancy as having their heads attached to another body. Three wives we spoke with said violence grew out of their irritability which began when they became pregnant.

Mrs. (19):   He hit me one time when I was pregnant—but I was in such a nervous condition all the time.

Discussions of pregnancy often indicate that the biochemical changes which women experience cause them to become more critical of their husbands' behavior. For instance, pregnant women become more fearful of being in a car and criticize their husbands' driving more often (Colman and Colman, 1973: 20). Thus, the changes in their bodies often cause pregnant women to "pick" on their husbands which can lead to conflict. In addition to irritability, these wives mentioned that they became depressed by having to stay home all the time and because they perceived a growing lack of sexual attractiveness.

PRENATAL CHILD ABUSE

Three of the wives who were hit when pregnant reported that the beating was followed by a miscarriage while a fourth wife told that the child born after the beating was handicapped. Whether on a conscious or subconscious level, violence towards a pregnant wife may be a form of prenatal child abuse or filicide. Mrs. (80)'s comments give at least some evidence to support this claim.

Mrs. (80):   Oh yea, he hit me when I was pregnant. It was weird.

> Usually he hit me in the face with his fist, but when I was
> pregnant he used to hit me in the belly. It was weird.

It may not have been just weird, it may have been her husband's attempt to terminate the pregnancy and relieve him of the impending stress of yet another child.

Although we may be ascribing more cognitive processes than are actually in play, we believe that for many families violence which brings about a miscarriage is a more acceptable way of terminating an unwanted pregnancy than is abortion. On one hand we know that there is still considerable controversy over the moral and legal aspects of abortion, even after the Supreme Court ruling of 1972 which for all intents and purposes legalized abortion. On the other hand, research on violence indicates violence is typical of family relations and is often normative in family life (Steinmetz and Straus, 1973b, 1974; Straus, Gelles and Steinmetz, 1973; Gelles, 1974; Schultz, 1969). Consequently, violence which terminates a pregnancy may be more acceptable socially, morally, and even legally than is an abortion.

DEFENSELESSNESS OF THE WIFE

Howard Kaplan's work on aggression points out that aggression is more likely if the other person (the victim) is perceived as unwilling or unable to retaliate (1972: 610). Thus, pregnant wives may be vulnerable to violence because their husbands view them as unable or unwilling to retaliate because of their changed physical condition. Although we cannot know whether this is the case from our limited data, it is possible that just by being vulnerable to attack, makes the violence a more likely outcome to family conflict than other possible outcomes.

Implications

Our exploratory examination of this issue suggests that violence during pregnancy is much more common than anyone has suspected. There are hints in the findings that violence towards pregnant women is not just an individual aberration of aggressive husbands, but rather grows out of the stress of the situation, and is compounded when the family has other preexisting (i.e., to the pregnancy) stresses.

Furthermore, if our assumption about violence toward a pregnant wife being prenatal child abuse is correct, then this violence may serve as an indicator or predictor of future abuse of children in these families. Dr. Eli Newberger of the Children's Hospital Medical Center in Boston has found that child abuse and family stress are highly related. In addition, he has noticed a number of cases of women who were beaten when pregnant showing up in his cases of child abuse. These findings indicate that intrafamily violence arises as a result of stress and severe frustration and that locating a family where a pregnant wife has been assaulted could serve as an indicator of this family's use of physical aggression as a response to stress and the likelihood of future occurrences of violence towards children.

POLICY IMPLICATIONS

If, as we think, the generative sources of violence towards a pregnant spouse are similar to the sources of conjugal violence and child abuse, then the policy implications of this finding are similar to those proposed to deal with husband-wife violence and violence towards children (Gelles, 1973; Newberger, Haas and Mulford, 1973). Some suggested strategies of dealing with violence and pregnancy follow:

(1) *Planned Parenthood*. It is a known fact that unwanted children are the most frequently abused children (Gelles, 1973: 617). We have also seen that many wives are battered during their pregnancy because they are carrying unwanted or unplanned-for children. Therefore, one of the initial steps in formulating a strategy of intervention in cases of violence towards pregnant women is to provide an avenue to prevent or ease the stress of an unwanted pregnancy. Effective planned parenthood programs, dissemination of birth control devices, and the removal of legal and social stigma of abortion are all steps in the direction of reducing the likelihood of stressed pregnancies ending in attacks on the pregnant wife by her husband. This is particularly important because of the danger the assault poses to the unborn fetus. A recent essay published in Britain (Mindout, 1974) discussed the danger of mental retardation in a child due to its mother being beaten when pregnant.

It should be stressed at this point that the problems which are associated with unplanned or unwanted children are serious enough to mandate the inclusion of material on the need for planned parenthood and the alternatives to unwanted children in family life education curricula.

(2) *Preparation for Parenthood.* As we cited earlier, pregnancy produces a number of chemical and emotional changes in a woman. These come as a surprise to her and a particular surprise to her husband. If neither partner knows about, or understands the origin and nature of these changes, there is the real possibility of severe conflict and stress arising in the family. The preparation for childbirth classes that are held in conjunction with the teaching of natural childbirth serve to teach both potential mothers and fathers about the various aspects and changes that go on in a woman during the term of her pregnancy. Because both spouses are aware of these factors they are likely to be better able to cope with the changes and new irritabilities and stresses posed by pregnancy. One problem is that these classes in prepared childbirth typically do not commence until the seventh month of pregnancy, long after the changes have occurred and had their effect on family life. Thus, it would be helpful, particularly for families already under stress (unemployment, sporadic employment, economic problems, housing difficulties, and so forth) to enter into preparation for childbirth classes early into the pregnancy—as early as possible. Furthermore, these sessions are critically important for the husband, to inform him about what he can expect to occur during the next nine months.

As in the case of planned parenthood, information which prepares men and women for the problems and stresses of pregnancy are of such critical importance to family functioning that they ought to be included in family life education courses. Material which outlines the biological process of pregnancy ought to be supplemented with information which points out the likely problems and social stresses that occur in households during the term of pregnancy. Some of the articles previously cited (Colman and Colman, 1973; Congdon, 1970; LeMasters, 1957; Rossi, 1968) would be most suitable readings in this area.

(3) *Family Crisis Centers.* One major feature which contributes to intrafamily violence is that there typically no escape from the scene of stress and conflict. Small arguments can escalate into knock-down, drag-out fist fights because there is no place to flee for refuge (Gelles, 1974). In the case of violence towards a

pregnant wife, this is an important factor because of the wife's defenselessness. Thus, one policy which can be developed is to establish family crisis centers and crisis telephone numbers. Many wives I talked with said they stayed in the house and were beaten because they had no place to go. If there is some shelter they can go to, they can leave the scene of the conflict in order to let the conflict die down or to be in a neutral setting while others try to intervene with services or through legal means to cope with the situation which led to the potential for violence.

(4) *Basic Needs.* It is obvious to all family practitioners that for a family to function adequately there are certain basic needs which must be fulfilled—medical care, dental care, nutritional needs, housing, and so forth. But in the case of a family where the wife is pregnant, these needs are more critical because of the obvious presence of the potential new member. Thus, a family of two might have certain objective needs during the pregnancy that are being met, but they are more concerned with their future needs because of the addition of the baby. The three-room apartment which is suitable for a two-person family, may be thought by that family to be too small for three. The practitioner or counselor must be aware of and help to provide for a pregnant family's future basic needs as well as their present basic needs.

This topic is too new and I am too inexperienced in the area of family counseling to add further to this preliminary discussion of the policy implications of the findings on violence and pregnancy. But it is important to note that the services needed to deal with this problem will be a synthesis of those services designed for families experiencing conjugal violence, and families where children are abused.

Conclusion

The major contribution of this note has been to alert those involved in providing family services to a previously unrecognized problem in family lives—violence towards pregnant women. In addition this note points out an area which needs more research to provide better data on this issue.

In terms of providing family services and for developing policies of intervention in families where violence occurs, it is important to realize that the crisis and transitions of parenthood begin during the pregnancy and not only after the child is born.

Chapter 7

POWER, SEX, AND VIOLENCE:

THE CASE OF MARITAL RAPE

The Women's Movement in the 1970s has increased the sensitivity of women and society to two major crimes which women fall victim to: sexual assault and physical assault by their husbands. Victims of rape and battered wives have a great deal in common. For years these two crimes have been the most underreported crimes against persons in the criminal justice system. Additionally, battered wives and rape victims are often accused of "asking for," "deserving," or "enjoying" their victimization. Finally, in most cases of rape or physical assault by husbands, women who turn to the criminal justice system for assistance or relief are often maltreated or ignored by police, lawyers, and judges.

The purpose of this essay is to examine rape and physical violence together by analyzing the case of marital rape. The entire subject of marital rape, or sexual assault of wives by husbands opens up a host of controversies. First, the concept of marital rape

From Richard J. Gelles, "Power, Sex and Violence: The Case of Marital Rape." *Family Coordinator,* 1977, 26 (October): 339-347.

is one which does not exist legally. By legal definition, a woman cannot be raped by her husband, since the "crime" of rape is ordinarily and legally defined as forcing sexual intercourse on someone other than the wife of the person accused (Brownmiller, 1975; Gallen, 1967; Griffen, 1971; New York Radical Feminists, 1974).[1] Second, labeling sexual intercourse forced on a wife by a husband marital rape implies a major value judgment by the labeler concerning appropriate interpersonal relations between family members. Finally, if husbands force wives to have sexual relations, even accompanied by physical violence, do the wives or the husbands consider this behavior problematic or "rape"?

The essay begins by examining the controversies surrounding the study of marital rape. Next, the literature on rape is reviewed in order to summarize the facts known about rape which could be applied to the case of marital rape. The third section summarizes two sources of data which we use to shed some light on the incidence and social context of marital rape. The final section discusses further issues in the study of marital rape.

Does Marital Rape Exist?

The major question which must be addressed at the outset is, can we or should we investigate a phenomenon which, by legal definition, does not even exist? Rape has been defined conceptually as "any sexual intimacy forced on one person by another" (Media and Thompson, 1974: 12). A less objective and more culturally relative definition of rape is provided by Levine in his study of rape in the Gussi tribe. Levine defines rape as "culturally disvalued use of coercion by a male to achieve the submission of a female to sexual intercourse" (1959: 969). The dictionary definition of rape is "sexual intercourse with a woman by a man without her consent and chiefly by force or deception" (Webster's New Collegiate Dictionary, 1975). Thus, by dictionary definition, conceptual definition, and cultural definition, any woman can theoretically be raped by any man. Media and Thompson's definition (1974) implies that a man can also be the victim of rape by a woman, and research on homosexual assault in prison documents that men are raped by men (Davis, 1970). The criminal justice system modifies these definitions by not viewing forced sexual intercourse between husbands and wives as rape. The rationale for this appears to be that the courts view the marriage contract as requiring wives (and husbands) to have sexual relations with their spouses (Cronan, 1969). While the "duty" of sex is, in a legal sense, equally distributed in marriage, the compulsory nature of sexual relations in marriage works chiefly to the advantage of the male (Gillespie, 1971) because men are typically able to muster more physical, social, and material resources in their relations with their wives.

Given that marital rape does not exist legally, should we examine it as part of family behavior and as an aspect of marital violence? We believe that we should. The legal prescriptions which imply that the wife is the "property" of her husband (Griffen, 1971) and which give the husband the permanent right to sexual relations once the wife says "I do" (New York Radical Feminists, 1974) are a reflection of an ideology, not a portrait of reality. The law is a reflection of what behavior ought to be, not what behavior actually is. The fact that the criminal justice system is largely populated by males partially explains the fact that legal statutes reflect a "male dominant" view of family behavior. A case in point is the California Penal Code which requires that a woman be more injured than is commonly allowed for battery in order to press an assault charge against her husband (Calvert, 1974). The fact that the courts do not accept the concept of marital rape does not, in our opinion, mean that wives are not being raped by their husbands.

Because forced sexual relations between a husband and wife are not legally considered cases of rape, the question arises whether or not a wife herself views the incident as a rape. This is an empirical question which we will take up in detail in a later section of the essay, but it is likely that the majority of women who are physically forced into having sexual intercourse with their husbands do not consider this to be an incident of rape, a violent act, or a deviant act. Thus, if the victim herself is unlikely to view the behavior as rape, how can we discuss the phenomenon marital rape? In order to answer the question it would be wise to briefly analyze why a woman would not view physically coerced sex as rape. Our research on marital violence suggests that many victims of family violence (including abused children) do not view these acts as violence or as problematic. Women who have been beaten severely by their husbands often state that they "deserved to be hit," that they "needed to be hit," or that "husbands are supposed to hit their wives" (see Gelles, 1974; 1976; and Parnas, 1967). The fact that women are socialized to believe that violence between spouses is expected and normative, does not diminish the fact that women are often injured by their husbands in trying to redress these acts (see Field and Field, 1973; Truninger, 1971; Gelles, 1976). In analyzing forced sexual relations between spouses, we believe that the pervasive ideology of "women as men's chattel" has served to deny women the opportunity to perceive their own sexual victimization. We have chosen to discuss the issue of marital rape, irrespective of the wife's subjective perceptions of the behavior, because we believe this is a phenomenon which needs to be questioned and studied.

The discussion of the wife's perceptions of forced sexual intercourse and our rationale for choosing to investigate this phenomenon despite the fact that many women do not perceive themselves as rape victims raises the issue of the value implications involved in labeling the phenomenon rape. Rape is a perjorative term which connotes repulsive and violent deviance. Webster's New Collegiate Dictionary states that rape can also be defined as "an outrageous violation" (Webster's New Collegiate Dictionary, 1975). We have chosen to use the term rape in this essay for the same reasons we have decided to title our investigation "studies of violence between family members" and for the same reasons we have chosen to study abused wives. We believe that the area of violence between family members has long suffered from selective inattention (Dexter, 1958) both at the hands of social scientists and society in general. The plight of victims of violence between family members has been overlooked by students of the family, agencies of social control and social services, and the public at large. In order to rectify this situation, it often requires using an emotionally charged word to draw attention to this phenomenon. The history of research on abused children reveals that battered children were largely ignored until Henry Kempe labeled the phenomenon as The Battered Child Syndrome (Kempe et al., 1962). We have decided to label this essay an investigation of marital rape partly as a reaction to the discriminatory practice of not allowing a woman to protect herself from violent or physically coercive sexual intercourse at the hand of her husband, and in an attempt to draw scholarly and public attention to this issue.

Research on Rape

Because the law views rape as an act of sexual penetration of the body of a woman *not one's wife,* there are virtually no official statistics available on the subject of marital rape. Brownmiller alludes to the depiction of a marital rape on a television episode of the series "The Forsythe Saga" (Brownmiller, 1975) and Russell (1975) devotes a chapter of her book to a description of marital rape. Beyond these descriptive data and illustrations, there is little else one can locate which bears directly on the incidence or nature of marital rape. The lack of official statistical data is a direct result of the law not viewing marital rape as a crime. Peters (1975), for example, reports that none of the patients he treated for incestuous rape reported their assaults.[2]

There are two areas of rape research which bear on the case of marital rape. The first area is the study of victim-offender relations and the second considers the element of "power" as a component of sexual assault.

VICTIM-OFFENDER RELATIONS

The conventional wisdom concerning rape suggests that women are typically assaulted in dark alleys by strangers. The research which has been carried out on patterns of rape indicates that this conventional wisdom may be more myth than reality. Amir's research (1971) on patterns of victimization revealed that 48% of the rape victims knew the offender. Pauline Bart's (1975) examination of 1,070 questionnaires filled out by victims of rape found that 5% of the women were raped by relatives, .4% by husbands, 1% by lovers, and 3% by ex-lovers. Thus, a total of 8.4% of the women were raped by men with whom they had intimate relations. Bart's survey also found that 12% of rape victims were raped by dates and 23% were raped by acquaintances. Less than half of the victims (41%) were raped by total strangers.

Additional research on rape also reveals a pattern where victims were likely to know the offender or be related to the offender. Of the 250 victims of rape studied by the Center for Rape Concern at Philadelphia General Hospital, 58% of the rape victims under the age of 18 were assaulted by a relative or acquaintance. When the victim is a child, she is likely to be sexually attacked by her father—six of the 13 children were raped by their fathers (Peters, 1975).

The research on victim-offender relationships dispels the myth that the majority of women are raped by strangers. For the purposes of our focus on marital rape, the research results indicate that intimacy and sexual assault are frequently related. The women who are raped by boyfriends, dates, lovers, ex-lovers, husbands, relatives, and other men that they know *might* represent the tip of an iceberg which reveals a more extensive pattern relating intimacy with forced sexual relations.

POWER AND RAPE

A theme in much of the literature on rape is that rape is less a sexual act and more an act of power in the relations between men and women. Bart concludes, based on her analysis of questionnaires filled out by rape victims, that rape is a power trip, not a passion trip (1975). Brownmiller also perceives rape as a power confrontation. She views rape as an act of hostility towards women by men—rape is an attempt of a man to exercise power over a woman (1975). Seites (1975) agrees that rape is a sexual power confrontation. She postualtes that marital rape is an act where a husband can assert his power and control over his wife.

If rape is viewed more as an act of power than a sexual act, then we can examine marital rape by focusing on the power dynamics of the family. Goode (1971) has stated that all social systems depend on force or its threat, and that the family is no exception. Goode goes on to propose that the more resources individuals have, the more force they can command, but the less they will use that force. On the other hand, the fewer resources individuals have, the less force they can command, but the more they will use the force. Goode theorizes that men who lack sufficient resources to hold the socially prescribed dominant role in the family will use physical force to compensate for the lack of resources.

If Goode's resource theory of family violence is correct, then we can predict that men who command limited social/psychological, and verbal resources are likely to use more force on their wives than men who are well educated, hold prestigious jobs, and earn a respectable income (see O'Brien, 1971 and Gelles, 1974 for empirical data on this hypothesis). If rape is viewed as an act of violence and an act of power, we could deduce that men who have few social and psychological resources are likely to use an act such as marital rape to intimidate, coerce, and dominate their wives. Rape of wives might grow out of a husband's lack of verbal skills and an inability to argue equally with his wife, or it might be a means of the husband demonstrating how he can dominate his wife despite the fact that he is poorly educated or unemployed. In addition, because rape can be a degrading experience, some husbands may use this act to humiliate their wives and thus gain a degree of power and control over their spouses.

Research on Marital Rape

While the research on victim-offender relationships, on victims of rape, and on family violence allows us to speculate about marital rape, the research carried out to date allows no direct insights into the incidence or nature of the phenomenon. In order to provide some direct information on the topic of marital rape we attempted to gather data which would shed light on this phenomenon. This section reports on two investigations. The first was a survey of Rape-Crisis Centers which asked the centers to provide us information on the number of cases of marital rape they encounter and on specific aspects of these cases. The second investigation was part of a larger study of physical violence between husbands and wives (see Gelles, 1974; 1975c, 1976). The second investigation analyzed transcriptions of interviews with women who had been beaten by their husbands to see what information could be gleaned on the sexual aspects of the beatings.

The increased attention on the plight of victims of sexual assaults led to the establishment of Rape-Crisis Centers throughout the nation which provide legal, medical, and social services to victims of rape. In the spring of 1975 Joan Seites (1975) contacted 40 Rape-Crisis Centers which were chosen from a listing compiled by the Center for Women Policy Studies.[3] From the centers 16 completed questionnaires were returned (one questionnaire was returned because of insufficient address), a response rate of 40%.

The purpose of the survey was to determine whether or not cases of marital rape are reported to Rape-Crisis Centers, and if so, how many cases are reported. Of the 3,709 reported calls dealing with rape and attempted rape received by the 16 centers, 12 calls dealt with marital rape (.3%). This figure is low and comparable with Bart's finding (1975) that .8% of the victims of rape reported being attacked by their husbands.

Because Rape-Crisis Centers do not always record the offender-victim relationship, we cannot be sure that the 12 reported marital rapes fully represent the proportion of husband-wife rapes in the 3,709 calls which were handled. However, the data do reveal that at least some women are reporting instances of marital rape despite the fact that the law does not view forced marital sexual intercourse as rape and despite the fact that few women would view physically coerced sex at the hands of their husbands as requiring a call to a Rape-Crisis Center.

The questionnaires also asked the centers to discuss some of the aspects of the calls they received about marital rape. One agency reported that women complained that their husbands were coming home drunk and hitting them and then raping them. These callers were not asking for rape counseling, they asked for information about divorce. It would appear that because there are few agencies which are capable of providing counseling and assistance to battered wives (there were 6 Battered Wife Centers in the United States as of March 1976), that women who were beaten by their husbands seek help from the best known women's agency—Rape-Crisis Centers. Thus, wives may report rape and battering to centers in order to get some help in solving problems of marital violence.

The agencies which did provide information about cases of marital rape reported that raped wives were likely to be fearful of future assaults and were angry with their husbands. One agency provided a personal account of a woman whose husband attempted to rape her:

Almost 14 years ago, my first husband attempted to rape me. At the time, we were very close to being separated and I think he wanted to attempt to bring us closer, back together through a sexual act—he always maintained that that was his prime means of communication, how he felt the closest. At first I fought and when he attempted to smother me with a pillow, I panicked and become only concerned with how to get him to stop—I was afraid he was going to kill me. So I became totally unresponsive to him—wouldn't talk or anything and he eventually stopped tearing my clothes and pulling me and there was no intercourse. Because it happened in the context of a whole lot of bad things in our marriage (he had been violent to me once or twice before, but not sexually so), I didn't have any particular feelings at the time except relief that it was over. Very shortly thereafter, I left him. I never thought of the incident as attempted rape until almost 10 years later when I was walking away from a session of a women's group I was in wherein we had been talking about specific rape incidents that had occurred to some of the members. Until that time, I think I felt rape was of the stereotypic type of the stranger leaping out of the bushes and never thought of an incident like that occurring between people who knew each other—especially husband and wife, as rape. I think this is true of many married women—they have accepted society's dictum that a man has sexual access to his wife whenever he wants, whether she does or not. Thus, it never occurs to them that this could be a crime, a felonious assault, that this is, indeed, rape.

The questionnaires from the Rape-Crisis Centers provide some additional information on marital rape. First, although forced sexual intercourse may take place frequently between husbands and wives, most women do not view this as rape.

I know personally, not professionally, many women who have been raped by their husbands. Some file for divorce. Few consider the act rape, since they themselves consider themselves property.

Most women probably do not realize, or classify such actions as "rape" because they have been infused with cultural myths surrounding rape.

Many wives view themselves to blame for the incidents of forced sexual intercourse. The woman raped by her husband who was interviewed for Russell's book (1975) indicated that she thought the incident was partially her fault because she should have known not to get into the situation which led to her victimization. This kind of victim-blaming is common in incidents of rape where victims are thought to have brought on the assault through provocative behavior and being "in the wrong place at the wrong time." Victim-blaming by the victim is found in instances of

marital rape and marital violence (Gelles, 1974; 1976) as victims
of deviance in the family try to neutralize the stigma of the
deviance by blaming themselves for their husbands' behavior.

Lastly, as in cases of marital violence, women who are forced
into having sexual relations with their husbands are ashamed to
tell other people about this problem.

> The biggest issue we've noticed is that married women don't talk to
> each other about their sex lives to any extent and especially not about
> rape!

IN-DEPTH INTERVIEWS

Interviews with 80 family members on the subject of violence
between husbands and wives elicited some discussions about the
relation between sex and violence. A number of wives reported
being beaten by their husbands as a result of their husbands
becoming jealous over a suspected incident of infidelity. Husbands
also reported that their wives struck them over suspicions about
extramarital affairs (see Gelles, 1974: 82-85 and 147-148).

Although the questions asked in the course of the interviews did
not specifically pertain to the subject of marital rape, an analysis
of the transcriptions of the interviews identified four women who
discussed sex-related violence which could be viewed as instances
of marital rape or attempted marital rape. The most consistent
pattern found in the interviews with the four women was that
they felt that they were coerced or forced into having sex with
their husbands and that the husbands criticized the wives for not
being affectionate.

> Well, uh, he used to tell everybody that I was cold . . . he (came home)
> drunk or he had been out half the night. I didn't really feel like it
> (sexual intercourse). But we never argued about it. Usually he got his
> way because I wasn't about to go up against it.
> He was one of those—he liked to strike out a lot and hit you and a lot
> of that was based on sex . . . he thought that I was a cold fish—I wasn't
> affectionate enough. . . . Sometimes he took a shotgun to me.
> He was drinking . . . I know that was the problem—he said as far as he
> was concerned I wasn't affectionate enough—it (sexual intercourse) was
> anytime he felt like it—whatever time he came home—it was crazy . . .
> different hours.

What emerged from the interviews was that wives frequently did not want to have sex with their husbands because of the fact that their husbands were drunk, came home at odd hours, or were critical of their wives' sexual responsiveness. The husbands, however, appeared to believe that their wives should have intercourse with them on demand and that if they refused it was because they (the wives) were frigid. Moreover, husbands seemed to view a refusal of intercourse as grounds for beating or intimidating their wives.

In all four cases, the wives gave in to their husbands' demands rather than be physically forced into having sexual intercourse. Thus, the review of the in-depth interviews did not find an instance of a woman being violently forced into having sex, as in the case discussed previously in this essay or the case discussed by Russell (1975).

We have stated previously that one reason why so little attention has been directed towards forced sexual intercourse in marriage is the theory that this is not viewed as a problem by most wives. One interview indicated that forced sex was, indeed, viewed as problematic by at least one woman in the study. This woman explained that she often provoked her husband into physical fights by verbally taunting him after he came home intoxicated and demanding sex. She went on to state that her husband would beat her after these verbal assaults, she would cry, and he would drop his demands for sex. Thus, she viewed being beaten up as a more acceptable alternative to marital rape.

An analysis of the literature on rape, the survey of Rape-Crisis Centers asking about marital rape, and the examination of transcripts of interviews on marital violence only begins to scratch the surface of the topic of marital rape. There are numerous issues which ought to be considered in detail in further investigations of marital rape. We shall briefly discuss five issues where further consideration is needed.

(1) It is claimed that the family predominates in acts of violence ranging from slaps to murder and torture (Straus, Gelles, and Steinmetz, 1976). Although the official statistics on rape do not bear us out, we believe that a woman is most likely to be physically forced into having sexual intercourse by her own husband. Previous studies of marital violence (Gelles, 1974; Straus,

1974a; 1974b; 1976; Steinmetz, 1975) have not examined sexual violence in marriage. We think that an important aspect of future research on violence in the family would be a focus on acts of marital rape and acts of violence which involve the sexual suppression of women.

(2) A second issue which we feel needs to be discussed is the nominal and operational definitions of marital rape. The central question which needs elaboration is whether marital rape is an act which must be accompanied by physical force and violence, or whether the act *itself* is violent? Interviews with women who had been victims of violence indicate that most of these women submitted to sexual intercourse without being physically beaten. Because the intercourse was not accompanied by violence, these women did not view the behavior as rape, and instead focused on their husbands' drinking or staying out late as the main problems in the marriage. Because marital rape is technically legal and because women have traditionally been socialized to believe they are the property of their husbands, we would speculate that the only instances of marital rape which would be reported to Rape Crisis Centers, social service agencies, or social scientists would be those cases where physical violence is involved. Thus, the full extent of how many women are verbally coerced or intimidated into having sex against their wills with their husbands may remain an unknown.

(3) We have been able to glean some insights on marital rape from the research on victim-offender relations in cases of rape. One area where the research on nonmarital rape can provide no help in understanding marital rape is the consequences of the attack. Much of the research on rape goes into great detail on the aftermath of the attack and the affects on the victim. We believe that the consequences of being raped by a stranger or even a boyfriend are far different from being raped by one's husband. Peters (1975) who studied a number of cases of incestuous sexual assault, proposes that rape by a family member or relative produces different emotional consequences than rape by a stranger. Peters states that rape by a stranger might be physically dangerous, but rape by a relative or friend may be more disillusionary. Russell's presentation of a case of marital rape (1975: 71-81) illustrates this point. Mrs. Michel, who was raped by her husband

in front of bystanders, stated that she felt the rape was partially her fault. She broke out in hives the next day and felt humiliated by the incident. While we know about the reactions of women who were raped by nonfamily members, and we have some data on battered wives, we know little about women who are sexually assaulted by their husbands. The available data suggest that raped wives are neither masochists nor do they enjoy being sexually assaulted by their husbands (see Russell, 1975: 75).

(4) A discussion of rape or marital violence almost inevitably raises the question of whether there is an association between acts of violence and acts of sex. Faulk (1977) suggests that marital violence may sometimes be sexually stimulating in itself. He states that some wives report that their husbands want sexual intercourse soon after a violent outburst. Faulk goes on to report that it is uncertain whether the violence itself is sexually stimulating or whether husbands are trying to use sexual intercourse as a means of reconciliation. In addition:

> Some wives report that their clothes were partly torn off during the violence, and a few saw this as sexually motivated. It seems likely, however, that in many cases the clothes were torn off to prevent women from escaping [Faulk, 1977].

The little empirical research and theoretical discussion which focuses on the relationship between sex and violence support Faulk's contention that sex is not an intrinsic component of marital violence. An analysis of TAT responses of college students to ambiguous pictures reveal little association between sexual thema and violent thema in the stories produced (Gelles, 1975a). While women did not associate sex with violence in their fantasy production, there was a slight association in the stories produced by men. Steinmetz and Straus (1974) argue that there is little evidence for a *biological* association between sex and violence and postulate that sex antagonism and sex segregation in this society might explain the tendency to use violence in sexual acts.

The analysis of marital rape suggests that the association of sex and violence are means which husbands can use to dominate and intimidate their wives without fear of outside intervention. Because women cannot legally charge their husbands with marital rape and because acts of marital violence rarely result in successful prosecution of the husband, forced sexual intercourse and marital violence are two unsanctioned methods which husbands can invoke to establish dominance in their families.

(5) The final point for consideration concerns the nature of the law which denies women the right to charge or seek prosecution of their husbands for acts of marital rape. An obvious question which arises is, if marital rape exists, and it is a problem, should the law be changed to provide women avenues of legal recourse for redress in acts of marital rape? If we argue that yes, the laws should be changed, there are two problems which arise. First, if all wives could take their husbands to court for forcing them into having sexual intercourse, this might flood the court with intrafamily litigations. The already overburdened criminal justice system probably could not handle the large number of cases which it might have to process. Second, arguing for changing the law somehow implies that such a change would provide women with legal rights. The case of marital violence serves as a good reminder that giving a woman the *de jure* legal power to charge her husband with an illegal act does not necessarily mean that the police and courts will provide her with relief and protection. Although women can charge their husbands with physical assault, the chances of the courts intervening and helping her are quite slim (Gelles, 1976; Truninger, 1971; Field and Field, 1973). Any legal change in the area of marital rape would also have to be accompanied by social, attitudinal, and moral changes whereby society views the issue of marital rape seriously, refrains from viewing victimized wives as being masochists or really enjoying the rape, and conveys a willingness to intervene in family matters and provide real protection for victims of marital rape.

Conclusion

The available evidence on marital violence indicates that a number of women are forced into having sexual relations with their husbands through intimidation or physical force. Faulk's research (1977) identified cases where sexual intercourse was forced on a wife after her husband beat her. Other data point to the fact that despite the fact that marital rape is not possible in a strict legal sense, some women are talking about and reporting incidents of marital rape.

From a research point of view, we believe that the topic of marital rape is an important area of investigation for social scientists. Investigations of marital rape and subjective perceptions of forced sexual relations between husbands and wives (including instances where wives are forced into having sexual acts that they find repugnant) will provide valuable insights into the family, power relations in the family, and the range and nature of sexual activities in marriage. A focus on marital rape also tends to move this subject from the taken for granted into the problematic. This transition might serve to call into question the legal position of women and whether women ought to have broader legal rights in terms of dealing with their husbands. We conclude that the head-in-the-sand approach to marital rape is no longer acceptable for social scientists, members of the criminal justice system, or for women in this society.

NOTES

1. South Dakota became the first state to eliminate the spousal exclusion from the statute on rape. The 1975 Rape Law reads: "Rape is an act of sexual penetration accomplished by any person" Other states, such as Florida, do not specifically exempt married persons from rape prosecution (Silverman, 1976: 10). NB: As of January 1, 1979, Oregon, Iowa, Delaware, Massachusetts and New Jersey had removed the spousal exclusion from their Rape Laws. South Dakota placed the spousal exclusion back in the Rape Law in 1977.

2. Incestuous sexual assaults are not reported for other reasons, among which might be the victims' embarrassment.

3. A sample of 40 crisis centers was chosen from the listing. A questionnaire was sent to Rape-Crisis Centers in each state represented in the listing. If more than one Rape-Crisis Center was listed in a state, then a single center was selected based on the degree of professionalism and organization indicated by the name of the center. The sample, while geographically broad, is *not* a representative sample of Rape-Crisis Centers. Each center was sent a questionnaire with a self-addressed, stamped envelope. Only a one-wave mailing was used in this survey.

Chapter 8

THE TRUTH ABOUT HUSBAND ABUSE

It was inevitable that battered husbands would be discovered. Given what we know about violence and violent behavior, it would have been highly unlikely if there were no women who physically attacked their husbands.

The media has been aware of the problem of family violence for a long time, but they tend to cover the issue piecemeal. The sixties was the era of the battered child. In the early and midseventies, and at the prodding of feminists, the media brought battered wives out of the precinct houses, emergency rooms, psychiatric wards, consciousness-raising groups and the private horror of their bedrooms, and kitchens, and into the public eye—although the issue of battered wives was not always received as sympathetically as were the stories about battered babies. Many skeptics assumed women must "like" this violence, else why didn't they leave. Interestingly, in the late seventies, the media developed a new slant on the issue—battered husbands—a classic "man bites dog" story.

From Richard J. Gelles, "The Truth About Husband Abuse." *Ms.* magazine, 1979
© 1979 Richard J. Gelles

Most of the media "evidence" on the extent of battered husbands was drawn out of context from a national survey of violence in the family conducted by Murray A. Straus, Suzanne K. Steinmetz, Response Analysis, and myself, and funded by the National Institute of Mental Health. Steinmetz's study focused on violence between siblings; Straus focused on marital violence; while I examined violence between parents and children.

The survey was conducted in 1976. We interviewed a representative cross-section of 2,143 American families. Approximately half of those interviewed were men and half were women. Studying a topic as sensitive as family violence is quite difficult. After all, you can't simply arrive at a doorstep and ask, "have you stopped beating your wife?" The survey employed an interview that had been developed over a period of seven years. Each person was asked how they dealt with marital conflict and 18 items were listed as possible responses. Of the 18 items eight pertained to acts of physical violence (threw something, pushed, grabbed or shoved; slapped; kicked, bit, or hit with a fist; hit or tried to hit with something; beat up; threatened with a knife or gun; used a knife or gun). The researchers presented summaries of violence between spouses using two measures.

First, we found that 16% of American couples used at least one of these forms of violence during the previous year. Second, a "severe violence index" was prepared including only those acts which had the greatest potential of causing injury (kicked, bit, or hit with a fist; hit or tried to hit with something; beat up, threatened with a knife or gun; used knife or gun). When the severe violence index referred to violence towards women, it was called the "Wife Abuse Index." Although it was never so named, the index, when applied to violence towards men, could have been labeled a "Husband Abuse Index."

If one goes only by the preliminary data[1] it appears that men are at least as likely to be battered as are women. But the case is much more complex than the raw numbers.

One glaring omission in the reports on "husband abuse" was a warning that the survey on which the estimates of the incidence of husband beating was based did not ask about or measure the *outcome* of the specific violent acts. In other words, we knew what husbands and wives did to one another, but we did not know how many husbands or wives were actually injured as a result of the violence. Certainly, one would expect that if a 280-pound, 6 foot 5 inch husband punches his 5 foot 4 inch, 120-pound wife, he will do more damage than she (but in the survey they would be recorded as being equally violent). Thus, although men and women tend to use the same forms of violence on one another, men may well cause more damage than violent women.

There were good reasons not to measure the consequences of violent acts. For one, it was too difficult to measure accurately. Second, from a strict theoretical point of view, it was not worth the energy and time to measure. The study was primarily concerned with violence. We learned in our early studies that the outcomes of violent acts are often determined by chance, luck, aim, or random factors. However, when comparing the rates of "wife abuse" and "husband abuse", it is vital to assess those outcomes.

In the same way, if one were to rely exclusively on the numbers, it would again appear that men and women are equally dangerous in the home. Statistically, about as many men kill their wives as wives kill their husbands. But once more the context of family violence must be considered. Elizabeth Pleck et al., (1977) in a critique of Steinmetz's research (1977), point out that while husbands and wives kill one another with equal frequency, wives are seven times more likely than husbands to murder in self-defense. In my own research I found numerous cases of wives using violence exclusively for self-defense. It is important to note that self-defense can mean more than just responding to a violent attack. A number of wives used what I called "protective reaction violence" (named after the unique terminology designed during the Cambodia bombings in 1971). In the situation of protective reaction violence a wife will strike first (and hard) to protect herself from her husband if she believes she is about to be abused again. Moreover, many women engage in husband abuse to protect themselves from potential harm or other degrading or humiliating experiences. Recently, there have been numerous cases of women who have killed their husbands and have pleaded self-defense. One common thread which ran through these accounts was that most of these women were defending themselves from physical or sexual attacks from their husbands. In most of the 50 states a wife cannot file a rape charge against her husband. (The exceptions, as of January 1979, are Oregon, Iowa, Delaware, Massachusetts, and

New Jersey. Most recently, a woman in Oregon became the first woman to charge her husband with rape. The husband was found innocent. According to the *Women's Rights Law Reporter,* nine states allow wives who are separated or have filed for divorce to file charges of rape against husbands.) Legally, it would seem that a husband can do anything he wants to his wife sexually, so long as he does not leave broken bones or whip marks. The structure of the law means that women are faced with either submitting to any and all sexual demands, or trying to defend themselves as best they can.

A minor problem with the estimates of husband and wife abuse grew out of the commonly held belief that men were reluctant to acknowledge they were abused by their wives, that husband abuse was the most underreported crime in the nation. In terms of reports to police; that may be true, but in terms of men being willing to discuss their own experience with violence, such is not the case. In fact, our survey of physical violence in the American family found that men are *more* likely to report their own victimization than were women. When men were asked if they were victims of severe violence, 4.9% said yes. When women were asked if they abused their husbands, 4.2% said yes. In terms of violence which could be considered wife abuse, 4% of the women said they were abused while 3.4% of the husbands acknowledged committing severe acts of violence. There are a number of possible reasons for these discrepancies, but one is that men, being in a superior position in the family and society, are perhaps less humiliated by being hit and are more likely to admit it than their wives. Another possible reason is that women, tragically, are more likely (in our society) to accept violence against themselves as normal. One thing is for sure: the estimates of the extent of husband abuse have to be considered somewhat biased by the different willingness of men and women to remember and report violence in the home.

Focusing on numbers is only one trap that keeps people from coming to grips with the real issues of marital violence. Another is the use of the term "abused." Abuse is not a scientific term, it is a political term. Beyond the measurable questions of who does what to whom, how often, and with what consequences, the real issue is the social, political, and legal context of the violence. This becomes a question of victimization. When men hit women and women hit men, the real victims are almost certainly going to be the women.

The study of family violence is relatively new. Serious research on domestic violence has been going on for less than a decade. But, much of what passes for knowledge is actually stereotypic thinking. Our national survey of family violence uncovered an abundance of detailed and surprising information that is needed to illuminate the patterns of marital violence.[2]

For example, two of the more common bits of conventional wisdom about domestic violence are (1) violence is found in all social groups; and, (2) violence is confined to specific types of people—psychopaths, poor people, or blacks.

Our study did, in fact, find violence in all types of social groups. No one group, whether geographic, economic, or age was free of marital violence. But, the violence is not equally distributed—some families were more likely to be violent than others. We do not believe, nor can it be proven that only people with personality disorders are violent. On the contrary, our research has shown that personality disorders are not the causes of family violence.

Our examination of marital violence found that families living in large urban areas, minority racial groups, individuals with no religious affiliation, people with some high school education, families with low incomes, blue-collar workers, people under 30, and families where the husband was unemployed had the highest rates of marital violence. (These findings, however, must be interpreted with caution—*each one* requires a more detailed explanation than we can provide here—for instance high rates of violence among minority racial groups are probably more due to economic than racial factors.)

Our examination also revealed that families with four to six children had the highest rates of violence. Furthermore, the greater stress a couple experienced, the more violent they were. Last, in homes where husbands and wives shared family decisions, the rate of violence was the *lowest*.

Examining the social context and social consequences of marital violence, one finds that irrespective of the kind of hitting that goes on, women are much more likely to come out on the short end. In many cases of marital violence women are physically helpless. They are smaller, less likely to be trained in the use of weapons, and, in many instances they are pregnant and almost completely unable to adequately defend themselves. Our first study of marital violence (Gelles, 1974) found that *one in four women who were victims of violence were hit when pregnant.*

Legally, women are at a disadvantage. Police officers, prosecutors, and judges are most likely to be male. Many a battered wife has heard a police officer, attorney, or even judge mumble under their breath, "If I were married to her I would have done the same thing."

Socially, women are at a disadvantage. Violence is most common among young families where women have young children. These women are less likely to work, have an adequate income, and be prepared to leave their home to protect themselves. Many battered wives are trapped in violent marriages. Their only viable recourse may be to hit their husbands to defend themselves.

When we look at the total phenomenon of marital violence it is clear that the claim "as many men are abused as women" gives a totally inaccurate picture. Indeed there are men who are hit and injured by their wives. Perhaps as many wives hit their husbands as are hit by their husbands. But the real issue is that the social position of women in the family and society makes them much more vulnerable to the torment of violence.

Beyond the debate over battered husbands is the issue of the violent family. Millions of our families are time bombs of violence because they teach their members that one can, and often should, hit loved ones. Research on child abuse has shown that each year as many as 2 million children are physically battered by their parents. Research has also demonstrated that if a child is exposed to violence in the home and is the victim of parental violence, that child is quite likely—as much as 1,000 times more likely than a child raised in a nonviolent home—to grow up and use violence against a child or spouse. An *Associated Press* wire service report released in August, 1978 discussed the latest form of abuse— parent abuse. The story presented cases of teenage children beating and killing their parents. Again, this should not be such a surprise. If a small boy grows up being hit by his parents and sees his mother hit by his father, one could expect that by the time he was a teenager, he would have learned that hitting was an accepted part of family relations. Many a battered wife has divorced her violent husband only to be the victim of her teenage children's violence.

Is there anything that can be done about family violence? Can the pattern of violence being passed from generation to generation be broken?

The most important first step in coping with the problem of family violence is to protect the victims. In August, 1976 when *Ms.* magazine devoted a cover story to battered wives, there were perhaps 20 operating shelters in the United States (as opposed to 90 in Great Britain). Today, there could well be as many as 100 (no one really can keep accurate track, and the number grows each day). Compared to five years ago, 100 shelters is a great improvement. But consider that there are 2 million battered wives in need of help, then 100 shelters is a woefully inadequate number. When the idea of a shelter is suggested, some people say, "but our community is too small." Yet that same community, whose population may be under 3,000 will have an animal shelter for abused dogs, cats, and bunnies. Put simply, humans must have parity with the dogs and cats of the world. Each community with an animal shelter must have a people shelter.

But, people retort, shelters are expensive. That is true, but shelters are by far the most efficient dollar and labor investment in the struggle to help victims of domestic violence. Money is not available for shelters because politicians do not recognize domestic violence as an important problem. The U.S. House of Representatives defeated the Domestic Violence Assistance Act in May 1978. That bill would have provided 16 million dollars for research and services on domestic violence. Ironically enough, 16 million dollars does not even begin to pay the handtowel bill in federal buildings in Washington. It is a rounding error over at the Pentagon. The Ninety-Fifth Congress appropriated 16 million dollars to support the United States Olympic effort for the 1980 Olympics. Yet, it was too much to invest in protecting millions of citizens. (The Domestic Violence Assistance Act will be reintroduced.)

After you protect the victim, one has to start thinking about preventing violence. One of the most ruthless contributors to domestic violence is our society's tolerance and acceptance of many forms of violence.

Each day our children are exposed to a variety of messages which tell them that hitting other people is OK. Corporal punishment in schools is legally and morally accepted, and even mandated. People say, our children need more discipline, and confuse discipline with hitting. The PTA is worried about the effects of violence on television and compiles a list of the most violent shows. But if seeing violence on television contributes to violence, imagine what the impact of seeing violence in the classroom is. The PTA ought to think about listing the top 100 violent school systems and comparing that to the rates of violence of the children when they leave school for the streets.

Violence and the threat of violence are the messages which people grow up with. It is not surprising that children who experience harsh punishment at home are the most ardent supporters of capital punishment. At the bottom of the tangled web of violence is the truism that violence does indeed beget violence. Each generation of children brought up on violence is another generation of potential child, wife, and yes, husband beaters. Accept violence as an inevitable part of raising children and accept the consequences of a violent society. Reject violence as a normal part of family life and you begin to see that it is possible to raise a healthy, happy, and well-behaved generation which does not see the fist as the solution.

NOTES

1. The *preliminary* analysis of the severe violence data showed that 3.8% of American wives had been victims of at least one of the *severest forms* of violence. Additionally, 4.5% of American husbands were found to be victims of at least *one form* of severe violence. Projecting these data to the 47 million couples in the United States, it was estimated that 1.8 million wives are battered by their husbands, while more than 2 million husbands are battered by their wives.

2. The complete findings will be presented in the forthcoming book, *Behind Closed Doors, Violence in the American Family* by Murray Straus, Richard Gelles, and Suzanne Steinmetz, to be published in September 1979.

Part III

STUDYING FAMILY VIOLENCE

Introduction

STUDYING FAMILY VIOLENCE

When we began our investigations of the extent, patterns, and causes of violence between family members we were immediately struck by the fact that there was no coherent body of literature which constituted a knowledge base. There were numerous research reports authored by psychiatrists, social workers, and physicians on the subject of child abuse and neglect. There were very few essays on the topic of spouse abuse or the use of violence between marital partners. There were two plausible reasons for the knowledge gap. First, family violence could have been rare and those few cases of violence or abuse could be explained as a function of mental illness. The other plausible hypothesis was that family violence was quite extensive, but social scientists had failed, for various reasons, to investigate it.

The first few tentative probes into the extent of violence between family members (Straus, 1974b; Steinmetz, 1971) cast doubt on the hypothesis that there was no research because there was no violence. After the first few studies it became obvious that one reason why there was little research on family violence was that investigators either did not want to ask questions such as "have you stopped beating your wife or child ..." or felt that they could not obtain reliable and valid answers to such questions.

As we became convinced that the family was a violent institution and as we pushed forward with larger and more ambitious studies, we were continuously told that we could not expect to carry out sound empirical research on family violence because we could not expect people to answer our sensitive questions. But people did answer our questions—with a startling degree of candor and detail. Whereas, we were afraid that people would slam their doors in our faces, we found that many of the subjects we approached would talk to us far beyond the one hour we expected the interviews to run.

The first essay in this section, "Methods for Studying Sensitive Family Topics" is designed as a road map to provide aid to those who want to study sensitive topics such as family violence. We review the major problems and possible solutions in conducting sensitive topic research, including sampling, rapport, validity, and reliability.

The second essay is a methodological critique of some of the current forms of research on child abuse and family violence. We argue that some of the methods and some of the data analysis procedures serve to extend, rather than explode myths about abuse and violence.

In large part, the essays in this section are designed to show that sound scientific investigations of family violence can be carried out and researchers need not close down certain research options in advance.

Chapter 9

METHODS FOR STUDYING SENSITIVE FAMILY TOPICS

A dilemma confronts social scientists seeking to examine behavior when long-standing taboos exist against discussing such behavior publicly or with one's intimates. Sensitive issues or "taboo topics" (Farberow, 1966) bid for scientific attention for a number of reasons: they are intrinsically interesting, allow scientists to analyze and refute conventional wisdom or myths about human behavior, concern regions of human behavior where knowledge gaps exist, and are fundamentally important for improving our insight and knowledge about less sensitive social phenomena. At the same time, sensitive issues and taboos pose major obstacles for researchers.

Special Problems in Sensitive Area Research

Sensitive issues aside, the family is a complex and difficult social institution to study. For one thing, families are made up of individuals occupying multiple statuses and enacting multiple roles. Thus, a researcher who interviews a family member or requests that a member of a family fill out a questionnaire is collecting data from an individual who is at the intersection of many and varied roles (mother, wife, worker, daughter, sister, and the like). Second, "family" as a group or institution is as much a matter of subjective perception as it is an objective group membership. As Laing (1971) put it, "to be in the same family is to feel the same 'family' inside." And because a number of individuals make up a family, there are numerous subjective perceptions of family interactions and individuals. Thus, while there may be a shared "reality" of family, which can be studied (Berger and Kellner, 1964), there are also varying subjective perceptions depending on whether the observer is a "son," "father," "mother," and the like.

The numerous roles, statuses, and shared perceptions complicate research into the family, but there are two additional facets of the family that influence the study of sensitive topics. First, the family is essentially a private institution (Aries, 1962; Laslett 1973). Second, the family is an intimate social group.

PRIVACY

A major contingency in the field of family studies is that the family is a private institution. As such, most relevant family interaction takes place behind closed doors, out of sight of neighbors, friends, and social scientists. In order to study the family, most social scientists have made use of methods and instruments that allow them to penetrate the walls of the family without actually going into the home. The majority of all social scientific research on the family involves the use of interviews and questionnaires. Less than 1% of current research on the family employs observational techniques (Nye and Bayer, 1963). The reliance on survey methods rather than field methods in the study of the family also indicates that the private nature of the family makes it difficult to employ standard observational or participant observation techniques. The exceptions are few, and often involve a researcher moving in and living with a family, as Jules Henry did in his study of families with psychotic children (Henry, 1971).

While researchers have been allowed entrance into families to study global family interaction patterns and some researchers have moved in as boarders in households while pursuing community studies (Whyte, 1955), it would be difficult to gain admittance into a household for the purposes of observing child beating or varieties of sexual behavior. Moreover, the private nature of the family also means that certain rooms are devoted to specific activities. A researcher might be allowed into a home, but not into the family's bedroom or bathroom for the purpose of making observations.

In conclusion, the private nature of the family puts a premium on methods that require the family member to recount previous histories or events and report them on a questionnaire or in an interview. Even these methodological approaches encounter the problem of intimacy, which blocks access to certain behavioral and attitudinal domains.

INTIMACY

Unlike other social groups, family structure arises out of intimate interactions. The special nature of intimate relationships tends to produce strong pressures against discussing family matters with outsiders. Parents often reprimand children for discussing their family matters with school counselors, friends, and neighbors. The tendency to view family matters as sacred, private, and intimate leads many individuals to take an adamant stand against uninvited intrusions by social scientists, market researchers, and the like.

Sensitive Topics

One of the most discussed sensitive issues in the past few years has been *child abuse.* This topic became a focal issue in the early sixties—propelled by a groundbreaking essay by Kempe and his associates (Kempe, et al., 1962). But, by 1978, we still do not have an adequate understanding of child abuse. Research which tests hypotheses is rare, causal models are overly simplified, and theory building research is often inadequately conceptualized. Moreover, there is currently no reliable estimate of how many children are abused and neglected each year in this country—a situation that led the Office of Child Development/National Center on Child Abuse and Neglect to sponsor a National Incidence Study of Child Abuse and Neglect beginning July 1, 1976.

A related topic is *spouse abuse.* As with child abuse, scant information exists on incidence and causes. But, even more importantly, spouse abuse had been ignored to such a degree that almost no descriptive data exist on this topic.

A third issue is *sexual abuse and incest.* Most textbooks on the family devote numerous pages to discussing the extent and nature of incest taboos in various societies and cultures. These discussions attempt to explain why such taboos exist and what form they take. The examination of taboos related to incest masks the fact that exceptions to the rule abound. Huerta (1976) has discussed reasons why incest has been a neglected topic for social scientists, and the fact that incest and sexual abuse remain the most underresearched aspects of child abuse and child neglect.

Of the 50 states, 49 have laws on the books that prevent a wife from filing a rape charge against her husband (Gelles, 1977); consequently, the issue of *physically coerced sexual relations* between husbands and wives has remained hidden from public view and from the research community. Occasional newspaper accounts of women who have slain their husbands because of demanded sex or sex acts that the wives found repugnant testify to the importance of the issue, but we still have no idea about the incidence and nature of this side of family relations.

While the topic of premarital sex has been reasonably well researched (Hunt, 1973; Kinsey, Wardell, and Martin, 1948; Reiss, 1960), sexual relations within marriage appear to be underresearched in comparison.

There are numerous other sensitive topics that can provide new and fundamentally important insights into the nature of family relations. In fact, one method of uncovering such sensitive issues is to monitor the popular literature forums in which personal problems are discussed. Columns such as "Dear Abby" and "Ann Landers," along with the personal columns found in magazines such as *Redbook, Good Housekeeping,* and *Woman's Day,* provide informative insights into the backstage areas of the family. An example of how this type of material can stimulate research was related by a colleague who read an article in a women's magazine by a woman who was married to a homosexual. In discussing this with friends, our colleague learned that the same phenomenon was much more common than he first had realized; he was directed to someone who had experienced it and was willing to talk about it at length.

It would appear that there are many issues that constitute important social problems and provide important insights into the fundamental nature of the family, but have yet to be investigated. Furthermore, there appears to be an abundance of information and data available on these topics once the research community can overcome the major obstacles and hurdles of sensitive topic research in the family.

Methods of Studying Sensitive Issues

SAMPLING

The first problem faced by those who study sensitive family topics is to locate data sources and cooperative subjects. This problem is exacerbated by the low base rate of most sensitive phenomena. If one were to attempt a study of the incidence of child abuse (assuming a base rate of .005) and wanted a confidence level of 95%, the needed sample size would be 76,448 people. At $40 per interview, the cost of the study would exceed 3 million dollars!

Unless a researcher is focusing on an issue with a presumed high base rate, or has unlimited capital, most sensitive issue research on the family will need to employ nonprobability sampling.

When employing nonprobability sampling, researchers require techniques that will produce a sample in which the informational payoff is the highest and in which cooperation is not likely to be a major problem. Some of the sampling techniques used to investigate taboo topics follow.

Group sampling. Group sampling was the technique pioneered by Kinsey and his associates (Kinsey, Wardell, and Martin, 1948) in their study of sexual behavior. The Kinsey researchers were able to use group sampling because they did not have to concern themselves with the problem of low base rates of the behavior in question. In studying such issues as wife beating, incest, and the like, the use of any functioning group as a sampling unit might not be particularly helpful. However, there are specialized functioning groups where group sampling would be an aid in reaching potential subjects. Self-help groups such as Alcoholics Anonymous, Parents Anonymous (for child beaters), and certain women's groups might provide a number of subjects for research into sensitive issues.

The major drawback of this sampling procedure is that it would identify a particular subportion of the population under study. People who abuse their children and admit to it in a self-help group are thought to be quite different in terms of social and personal characteristics than those individuals who do not admit their abuse of children to others or themselves.

Snowball sampling. Snowball sampling, employed in studies of drug use (Goode, 1969), homosexuality (Humphreys, 1970), and professional gunmen (Polsky, 1969), facilitates research on sensitive issues because it allows the researcher to begin with one or two contacts and branch out to a wider sample of people. For instance, in the marriage of a woman to a homosexual mentioned earlier, the one case was able to identify a number of other women who had similar experiences; in a short time, a number of people were discussed who had experienced this problem. Our research on family violence (Gelles, 1974) (which did not employ snowball sampling) often involved interviews with family members who discussed friends and relatives who had experienced violence in their marriages. It is likely that almost any topic is amenable to a form of snowball sampling.

A drawback of snowball sampling is that it taps individuals and families who are immersed in social networks. Some sensitive topics are not particularly suitable for this type of sampling. For instance, the literature on child abuse states that people who abuse their children are often socially isolated from friends and relatives. It would be difficult to use a snowball method of sampling when social isolation is a causal factor of the behavior in question.

Neighbor informant. In 1965 the National Opinion Research Council administered an interview, directed by Gil (1970), which asked subjects if they ever physically injured their children. Of the 1,520 subjects, 6 answered in the affirmative. The survey also asked whether the subjects knew of neighbors who had physically injured their children. Regarding the question, 45 answered in the affirmative, and Gil projected this to an estimate of between 2.53 and 4.07 million children physically abused each year (Gil, 1970). This technique of estimating the incidence of child abuse has become known as the "neighbor informant technique." Basically, the technique acknowledges the problems of reliability and validity in getting people to self-report illegal or deviant behavior. This problem is overcome by getting some outside source who knows the family to report on behavior within the family unit.

While the neighbor informant technique is strong in estimating the incidence or prevalence of certain sensitive issues, it has two major drawbacks. First, it is suitable for particular neighborhoods and subcultures. Where neighborhoods are marked by physical closeness and social openness, the neighborhood informant technique is suitable. However, where physical closeness is low and privacy of family interaction high, neighbors may be able to aid in establishing incidence rates for particular phenomena, but the private and intimate nature of family units makes neighbors poor judges of certain familial qualities such as power or authority. Moreover, many neighbors are probably unable to provide accurate information about important social indicators such as education and age of their neighbor.

Family informant. When a neighbor or someone outside the family has too little knowledge of what goes on in the home to aid the research project, an investigator might make use of an informant *inside* the family. This technique samples family members who provide information about what goes on among the other members of the family. Straus (1974a, 1974b, 1977b) and Steinmetz (1974) surveyed college students and asked them to answer questions about violence in their families during their last year at home (senior year in high school). This technique allowed the investigators to get some insight into the level of intrafamily violence and the causal variables associated with family violence.

While college students are captive audiences and have more knowledge about their own family than do neighbors, there are some limitations to this sampling procedure. First, as Landis (1957) and Berardo (1976) pointed out, there are real problems with the overreliance on college students as research subjects. College students represent a narrow segment of the population. By using college students to study family life, we restrict our ability to generalize about marriage and family life (Berardo, 1976). Second, family informants might have limited knowledge about their own family life. They are unable to report about their parents' marriage during the early years (before they were born or when they were young), and they may have been sheltered from certain aspects of their family life. Taboo topics, by their very nature and sensitivity, may have been shielded from the children. Nevertheless, family informants are a lot closer to the core of family interaction than are neighbors or others who might be asked for information.

IDENTIFYING SUBJECTS FROM PUBLIC AND PRIVATE RECORDS

When a researcher wishes to investigate an issue in family relations but cannot use any of the previously mentioned methods of identifying and locating subjects, there are other methods that can be employed. Paradoxically, while the family is our society's most private institution, numerous transactions between family members become matters of public record. There are a number of public documents that can be used to identify and locate potential subjects for the study of sensitive issues.

Police records. Most police departments keep logs of all police department activities. These logs, while often crudely kept, are usually open for public inspection (as with most organizations, police departments vary in their desire to cooperate with social scientists wishing to use "public" records). Using the records of one police department to identify families where police officers had intervened in "family disputes," we developed a sample of 20 families who had been visited by police officers (Gelles, 1974, 1975a, 1975c). In addition, some families were identified by examining the police log to identify cases where family members filed complaints of assault against another family member. The method of using police records, while allowing for the location of families, has some drawbacks. First, the method depends on the cooperation of the department chief. Second, an officer usually has to be present to assure that no juveniles would be identified in the process of screening families. Finally, police logs are far from the most accurate sources of data—addresses, names, and dates are often in error and a considerable amount of time can be wasted tracking down addresses that are nonexistent or inaccurate.

Police calls. The problem of getting cooperation from police officials often makes using official police records impossible. An alternative, which does not require cooperation, but which capitalizes on the new CB radio fad, is to monitor the radio calls of police departments. Although this technique is time-consuming, it can yield a sample of families where disputes have taken place, where assaults occur, where child abuse is suspected, and where other matters requiring police attention occur. This method is dependent on being able to secure the operating frequencies of police departments and being able to decipher the codes used. The problem of faulty addresses and inaccurate information still prevails in this technique of locating families or individuals.

Newspapers. Newspapers (depending on region and area served) often provide interesting and informative material on families. We have examined a number of local and regional papers and have found a wealth of information that might be relevant for selecting cases for research on sensitive family topics. Some papers, for instance, list local police activities for the day or week. These listings would aid in locating families in conflict or those with particular attributes (quarrels, violence, and the like). In addition, papers that publish legal notices contain information of interest to social scientists. Listings of divorces and divorce decrees are published in many papers. A recent issue of *The Providence Journal* published divorce settlements that included statements that restraining orders had been issued against husbands seeing or visiting their families. Our research on family violence indicated that such restraining orders typically grow out of a wife's complaint that she or her children have been physically abused by the husband.

Private agencies. Private agency case files are confidential information. However, if a researcher can work out an agreement with an agency to aid in research, agency records can become sources of subjects. In our own research on family violence, we worked out an arrangement with a private social work agency by which to contact subjects. We told the agency what our research objective was and what type of subjects we needed. The agency then screened their files, and contacted subjects for their permission to be interviewed. When permission was granted, we interviewed families that the agency suspected of using violence on children. Studies of remarriage, multiproblem families, family conflict, child neglect, and the like could all use this method of locating families for research projects.

In addition to helping locate families for research, private agencies can be the primary sources of data on families. During our research on marital violence, we were interested in the topic of marital rape. The problem was that, because women cannot file a rape charge against their husbands, data on this issue are nonexistent. Interested in learning about the incidence and nature of physically coerced sex in marriage, we opted for surveying rape crisis centers and asking them what proportion of their calls came from women claiming to be raped by their husbands. We also asked what the agencies knew about this issue. The data helped us gain some insight into this previously uninvestigated topic (Gelles, 1977).

Advertisements. A final method for locating subjects is to place an advertisement in a magazine, newspaper, or professional journal stating what the research project involves and requesting people who desire to be subjects to contact the investigator. This technique is often facilitated by offering to pay subjects for their time. Prescott and Letko (1977), through an advertisement in *Ms.* magazine, located 40 women who were willing to fill out a questionnaire on wife beating. The drawbacks of this method are obvious, because many people may respond to the advertisement as a lark. The representativeness of subjects located using this procedure is typically unknown.

DATA COLLECTION: AFTER RAPPORT WHAT?

Once a sample of family members has been obtained, the next major problem facing the investigator is to obtain valid and reliable data from the subjects. When the topic under investigation is sensitive and emotionally charged, research subjects may be embarrassed to discuss the issue; they may perceive "demand characteristics" of the instrument or situation (Orne, 1962) and respond in a socially desirable manner; they may be insulted by the researcher's technique, approach, or questions and refuse to continue; or, as was feared by Humphreys (1970), the researcher who asks the wrong question may conclude the research as the target of a series of beatings by subjects.

The literature on research into sensitive issues is limited to discussing the advantages of developing "rapport" with subjects in order to minimize the above-listed risks and to maximize validity and reliability. However, rapport building is such an intricate interpersonal task that many potential researchers are either scared off by the prospect of having to build rapport, or proceed willy-nilly into the investigation, overly dependent on their ability to get along with people.

Interviews. Perhaps the most difficult part of any interview on a sensitive topic is the point where the researcher has to ask the respondent the key question or questions under consideration. No matter how much rapport may have been built up in the interview situation, most interviewers are not overly anxious to ask questions on the order of "Have you stopped beating your wife?" Yet, this type of question is often crucial for the research.

There are a number of techniques for approaching and asking the more sensitive questions in research on the family. The first is a "funneling technique." This approach was employed in an exploratory study of intrafamily violence (Gelles, 1974). The technique was an unstructured interview. However, the flow of the interview was designed to direct the discussion towards the issue of family violence. The interview began with a general discussion of the subject's neighborhood, friends and their families, and conflict and problems in their neighbor's families. Then the focus of the interview turned to the subject's family. General questions about conflict and problems were channeled toward questions about fights and, ultimately, violence.

The funneling technique allowed the interviewer to establish rapport with the subject, while familiarizing the subject with the basic content of the interview. The discussion gradually was chan-neled towards the issue of violence, and in many situations the subject began to discuss violence without a direct question. In instances where violence was not discussed spontaneously, the interviewer asked the direct question concerning the occurrence of violence in the family. (The funneling technique is discussed in more detail elsewhere [Gelles, 1974].)

Conflict resolution technique. The funneling technique was highly adaptable to an unstructured interview. Such a technique may require modification for use in structured interviews with large samples. An example of a technique used in a sensitive area is the conflict resolution technique developed by Straus (1974b, 1979c) for research on family violence. This technique, designed for and first used with college student subjects, was adapted for and implemented with adults in a national survey of violence in families (Straus, Gelles, and Steinmetz, 1979). It consists of a list of modes of conflict resolution, ranging from discussing an issue calmly to using a gun or a knife. Each item asks if the mode was *ever employed* in the family and how often the mode was used during the past year.

The advantage of this technique is that it accomplishes in a structured format what the funneling technique accomplishes in an unstructured format—it funnels the interview from the least sensitive to the most sensitive questions. This funneling allows for the building of rapport and has the additional benefit of building the subject's commitment to the interview (*e.g.*, a subject may rationalize: "Well, if I answered that question, I can certainly answer this one.") Although the conflict resolution technique has been used only in family violence research, it is highly adaptable to other sensitive issue research on the family.

Random response technique. No matter how good the rapport between the interviewer and the subject and no matter how successful the funneling technique employed, the researcher will eventually have to ask questions such as, "Have you abused your child?"; "Do you and your wife engage in anal intercourse?"; "Have you ever molested a child?"; "Have you ever used a gun on your wife?" These questions are particularly important and, at the same time, particularly difficult to ask. Interviewers, no matter how well trained, will often balk at asking such questions or ask them in a manner and with an inflection that suggests a "no answer" from the respondent. Subjects, on the other hand, may be embarrassed or afraid of answering the questions.

One manner of dealing with this problem is the random response technique developed by Warner (1965). In the original design a spinner was used to randomly select statements of a sensitive character such as: "I have masturbated . . ." or "I have not masturbated." The subject used the randomizing device out of the researcher's sight to select one statement for response. Responses could only be "yes" or "no." The researcher, not having seen which question was selected, could not interpret the answer, and the respondent's privacy was protected. Because the random response model is based on Bayesian probability theory, the researcher could estimate population parameters from the responses (Fidler and Kleinknecht, 1977; Horvitz et al., 1975; Warner, 1965).

The methodological advantage of the random response technique is that it guarantees confidentiality for the respondent and reduces the amount of response bias due to evasion. The technique has been reviewed and tested by a number of psychologists and they confirm the utility of the technique as a method of collecting accurate confidential information on sensitive issues (Fidler and Kleinknecht, 1977; Horvitz et al., 1975).

The disadvantage of this technique is its conception of the role of an interview subject. An interview subject will have to be extremely trustful of the technique to cooperate. It may be that the technique works only with subjects who are too naive to believe they might be fooled and with subjects who have doctorates in statistics and believe the technique is truly random. All the rest of the subjects in between might be extremely skeptical of how "random" and anonymous the technique is.

Collaborative and conjoint interviews. A fairly common problem in all family research, and particularly important when studying sensitive topics, is the reliance of a large proportion of research enterprises on the information provided by a single family member. Studies of family violence (Gelles, 1974; Straus, 1974b) and studies of child abuse typically gather data by interviewing one member of a family. This technique provides a single perspective on the issue in question. For example, a wife might consider a slap an instance of wife abuse, while to the husband it may have been so insignificant that he would not remember it in an interview. The level and meaning of violence in that family will depend on who is interviewed.

A possible solution to the problem of single perspectives is the conjoint and collaborative interview. Laslett and Rapoport (1975) suggested that conducting repeated interviews with several members of the same family, by more than one interviewer, increases the internal validity of the research and is particularly appropriate for research on the more private and intimate character of family life. LaRossa (1976) stated that common problems with family research, such as (1) dependence on female subjects, (2) overuse of self-report measures, (3) heavy reliance on "one-shot" data collections, and (4) failure to treat marriage in a holistic manner, can be solved by employing a conjoint interview procedure. This method involves husbands as well as wives, yields behavioral as well as phenomenological data, allows for the in-depth analysis of the marital world, and uses the marriage system level of analysis rather than the individual respondent level.

While LaRossa (1977) was able to employ the conjoint interview fruitfully in his study of first pregnancy, we found that this procedure had serious disadvantages when it came to a study of family violence. Our study of intrafamily violence included four conjoint interviews (Gelles, 1974). During the course of these interviews, issues of conflict and disagreement arose and the couples began to argue and disagree over the "correct" answer to the question. We felt that conjoint interviews sometimes created conflict that might have boiled over into violence after the interviewer had left the house. While we had no evidence that this did or could happen, we felt that it was wiser to conduct interviews with a single family member (Gelles, 1974).

Observations. Direct observation or participant observation in studies of the family is time-consuming, expensive, and rare. In studies that collected data through direct observation in the home the sample size was small and the research focused on global interaction patterns in the family (Henry, 1971).

Research on sensitive family issues involves problems other than those of time, cost, and small sample size. It is unlikely that a family will allow an investigator to make direct observations of sexual relations, violence, incest, or other volatile and private subjects. However, observation can be used to collect some data on households where the behavior in question exists or families who would serve as comparison groups to the others in a sample.

Focused observations in the home enable the investigator to gather valuable behavioral data to complement data that could be obtained through interviews and questionnaires. LaRossa found that the conjoint interview is also an opportunity to collect behavioral data (1976). There are various situations in which focused observation could be employed. For example, if data on how family members cope with stress is desired, an investigator might want to conduct observations of family interaction during dinner time. Bossard and Boll (1966) found that meals in the kitchen or dining room serve as the focal point of family interaction. This is one time of day when most family members are in the same room for a period of time. Additionally, meals are often stressful situations in which conflicts and arguments can erupt and must be dealt with (Gelles, 1974). The disadvantage of this procedure is that families might present a false front during the course of the observation, thus preventing the observer from gaining an insight into the real nature of the family. This problem might be reduced by repeating the observations over time so that the presence of the investigator does not change the fundamental manner in which the family members interact with one another.

Projective techniques. One method that is particularly useful in studying controversial issues is the projective test (Selltiz et al., 1959). Projective techniques such as the Thematic Apperception Test, the Rorschach Test, the draw-a-picture test, and the complete-a-sentence test are presumed to allow the subject to project internal states onto objects and behaviors external to himself (Kerlinger, 1973).

Projective techniques have been used extensively in family research. Numerous studies use them when children are the subjects of research (Haworth, 1966; Kagan, 1958; Radke, 1946). Children's perceptions of their parents have been studied by using line drawings and doll play (Cummings, 1952; Kagan, Hosken, and Watson, 1961). Projective tests such as the TAT and completion projects have been used with adults to study family-related personality traits (Blum, 1949), attitudes towards family members (Lakin, 1957), and family power (Straus and Cytrynbaum, 1961). Additionally, entire families have been the subjects of projective technique research designed to study familial perceptions (Alexander, 1952), and the direction of aggression in families (Morgan and Gaier, 1956).

Other researchers have designed projective tests to test for specific traits in the family. Edith Lord of the University of Miami developed a projective protocol that portrayed misbehaving children. The protocol varied the type of misbehavior and the age of the child (by having size vary). Lord administered the protocol to test for punitiveness in parents to gain some insight into the causes of child abuse. We have used a TAT projective device to test for the association of sex and violence in the fantasy production of college students (Gelles, 1975a).

The obvious advantage of a projective device is that it is a nonreactive method of collecting data. A projective test disguises the true purpose of the research. On the other hand, projective techniques have been criticized for being so ambiguous that they reveal the internal states of the *scorer* rather than those of the subject. In addition, projective techniques concentrate on internal states and it is difficult to argue convincingly that one can predict external behavior from internal states.

Experimental design. Experiments designed to examine sensitive topics in the family are limited by ethical and moral considerations in regard to the types of experimental manipulation the sample can be subjected to. Clearly, a researcher could not ethically design an experiment in which the expected outcome was a parent beating a child. An additional limitation is that experiments using families as subjects typically involve some degree of observation. Because experiments are typically conducted in the controlled setting of the investigator's laboratory, the family members will be interacting in a context quite different from the privacy and familiarity of their homes.

These limitations notwithstanding, there are some experimental designs that are amenable to studying sensitive areas in the family. For instance, if a researcher was testing the hypothesis that stress was causally related to aggression, modes of conflict resolution, or child abuse, the researcher could set up a true experimental design (Campbell and Stanley, 1963) where the variable "stress" was manipulated. The "Simulated Family" or SIMFAM technique, which has been used in studying problem solving (Straus and Tallman 1971), has been found to be successful in simulating family crisis. By manipulating the "crisis," the investigator might be able to examine the effects of stress on family conflict resolution. Although one could not expect to observe behavioral violence, the investigator could use a projective technique to assess the families' levels of internal aggression in the crisis or "no crisis" situation.

The advantage of the experimental design is that it allows for an *explanatory* analysis of the sensitive issues. Although experiments have been criticized for lacking correspondence to the real world, methodologists have argued that a valid experiment can be carried out even when the experimental variable is "phenomenally differ-ent" from events in the natural setting, as long as the experimen-tally produced variable is "conceptually similar" (Rieken et al., 1954; Straus, 1969).

The disadvantages posed by experiments arise when the experi-mental variables are not truly parallel to the real world. For instance, a researcher studying child abuse would have difficulty arguing convincingly that the experimental condition of depriving a child of candy is conceptually similar to physically abusing that child.

VALIDITY

Perhaps the most persistent question raised in the study of sensitive topics is: "How do you know the subjects told the truth?" Researchers studying sensitive topics tend to assume that few people would respond that they *do* engage in morally or normatively disapproved acts when they actually *do not*. However, there is considerable concern that many people who engage in covert deviance or other emotionally charged behavior will not readily admit it to social scientists. Humphreys, in fact, suggested that covert deviants wear the "breastplate of righteousness" which offers a "holier than thou" presentation of self (1970).

Kinsey and his associates attempted to resolve the threat to validity caused by a "social desirability affect." Kinsey and his colleagues pioneered the "direct approach interview." The Kinsey researchers argued that the burden of denial should be on the respondent, and that the interviewer should not ask questions that make it easy to deny certain behaviors (Kinsey, Wardell, and Martin, 1948). Thus, the Kinsey group began each interview assuming that every type of sexual activity had been engaged in by the respondent . . . and asked questions such as, "When did you last masturbate?", rather than, "Do you ever masturbate?"

While there is a need for validation studies of the techniques used in research on sensitive topics, to date such studies are rare, and even proposals for validation studies are few and far between. Bulcroft and Straus (1975) carried out a validation study on the use of college students as informants on family conflict resolution. They found that, when the same conflict resolution scales were administered separately to students and their parents, there was a high level of agreement on the level of family violence.

The "nomination technique" (discussed in the sampling section of this essay) might be validated by using official records to cross-check whether the neighbor reported for a particular behavior (child abuse, wife abuse) is known to police or social workers in the community. While this method of triangulation (Webb et al., 1966) is applicable to behaviors for which there are legal proscriptions and agents of control delegated the task of dealing with the problem, the cross-check method of validation will be useless for validating results on other behaviors, such as marital rape.

Whatever the method of sampling selected and whatever form of data collection is employed, there will have to be attempts to validate such research if the results of research on sensitive family topics are to be taken seriously.

Additional Constraints

PROTECTION OF HUMAN SUBJECTS

Researchers who engage in studies of sensitive topics that are funded by the federal government encounter additional problems posed by the Department of Health, Education, and Welfare guidelines concerning the protection of human subjects.

The purpose of the guidelines is to protect research subjects from physical or psychological injury which might arise as a direct or indirect consequence of the subjects' participation in research. While these guidelines tend to be directed towards medical or drug-related research, they still apply to all federally funded projects that employ humans as subjects.

The major guidelines that influence social science research on the family are the provisions that call for the subjects to give "informed consent" assuring that they have been provided full explanation of the project, a description of the risks involved, if any, a disclosure of alternative procedures that might be used, and an offer to answer any and all questions concerning the project. Additionally, subjects must be informed that they can withdraw from the project at any time (for a detailed definition of informed consent, see *Federal Register,* May 30, 1974: 18917). Researcher proposals must also guarantee that potential risks to the subjects are outweighed by benefits and by the importance of knowledge to be gained from the research.

Earlier versions of the federal guidelines called for informed consent to be obtained, in writing, before data collection began. It is obvious that this poses some problems for research enterprises which depend heavily on the establishment of rapport and trust for valid and reliable evidence to be obtained. It would be difficult for researchers to get a chance to establish rapport if they had to begin the research by stating that they were asking questions to learn about wife abuse, sexual abuse, incest, and the like. Moreover, researchers who vowed that the data collected were to be kept strictly confidential would confront suspicious subjects if they asked them to sign their names to a legal form which might look like a release of information.

The potential problems posed by these guidelines have been alleviated by new interpretations and exceptions made by HEW officials, which allowed some researchers to obtain complete informed consent at the end of the interview, questionnaire, or observation. In addition, such consent does not always have to be in writing.[1]

A problem with informed consent does arise if the researcher desires to have legal minors (under 18 years of age) as subjects. If Children are to be the subjects of sensitive research, informed consent must be obtained from parents or guardians. In addition, the consent must be obtained prior to meeting with the child. This restriction virtually guarantees that children will not be subjects of research on sensitive topics. No researcher could guarantee that a child being asked to report on parents' sexual or violent behavior would not be at risk if the parents knew the content of the research. Parents might give informed consent but still intimidate the child physically or psychologically after the interview. We know of no federally funded research in child abuse that is gathering direct interview or questionnaire data from children, and we conclude that the regulations protecting human subjects have produced this situation.

Thus, researchers seeking federal funding for sensitive research must be aware that the federal guidelines and the disposition of college and university human subjects committees are factors that must be considered in any research design.

"HIRED HAND" RESEARCH

When research projects attempt to investigate emotionally charged issues in the family on a large scale, additional problems are created by virtue of having to employ other staff members for various parts of the project. Roth (1966) has listed and discussed the numerous problems involved in what he called hired hand research. He discussed "faking" of observations, collaboration among coders to make their results similar, interviewers completing interview schedules by themselves, and other problems. Large-scale research projects usually develop mechanisms to "catch" the cheaters on their staffs, including call-backs, comparing data of each interviewer to the group average, and reinterviews. Nevertheless, such controls are often absent or are not sufficient to locate instances where interviewers did not take time to develop sufficient rapport, where interviewers used certain intonations when asking questions which assured "socially acceptable" replies, and where research staff members discussed confidential interview material at cocktail parties (Roth, 1966).

Thus, while large research projects can produce larger samples of families with more ability to generalize from the data, the necessary division of labor in these projects and the necessity of using "hired hands" poses serious and often unimaginable risks to the validity, reliability, and ethical conduct of the research.

CONFIDENTIALITY

One of the major steps that must be taken in sensitive topic research is to guarantee to the subjects that all data being collected will be kept confidential. While it is relatively simple to mask the identities of subjects in the write-ups of case studies, and while statistical procedures used in analyzing and presenting data protect the identity of subjects, there is one potential problem that poses risks to the researcher and the subjects.

Although a number of social scientists have discussed problems associated with the right to keep information obtained in academic research confidential, and some researchers (Polsky, 1969) have offered to serve as test cases to determine whether a social scientist could keep his information private despite court orders, no clear precedent exists in this area.[2]

Thus, until the courts decide whether academicians can be granted immunity from having to release confidential data, researchers who engage in research that deals with illegal, sensitive, or taboo topics run the risks of being forced to turn over material they pledged would be kept confidential, of engaging in legal battles, or of spending time in jail for contempt of court.

Conclusion

The purpose of this essay has been to identify the problems associated with carrying out research on sensitive topics in the family and to list and discuss some solutions that can be and have been implemented in the course of research on child abuse, wife abuse, family violence, and sexual behavior. This has not been an exhaustive presentation of all the methodologies that have been employed to study all the taboo topics in the family. Rather, the essay has been largely influenced and confined to methodological insights gained from our own research on family violence (Straus, Gelles, and Steinmetz, 1973). Nevertheless, many of the issues and methods associated with our research program on family violence are applicable to other types of sensitive research in the family.

A goal of this essay is to aid in moving research on the family into new and unexplored areas of family behavior. We believe that numerous topics of interest and importance have gone uninvestigated because researchers were stumped by the problems of finding subjects, obtaining data, and establishing procedures for producing valid and reliable data.

The final question that arises is whether research on such topics should be done at all—irrespective of whether or not the major hurdles in doing the research can be overcome. Some may argue that the procedures and methods we discuss in this essay border on being unethical invasions of privacy of the family. In addition, some might feel that there are areas in the family that are too private and too sacred and should not be investigated by "snooping" social scientific "voyeurs." Deception, ethics, morality, and the sacred nature of the family as a social institution are often cited as reasons not to carry out research on sensitive topics.

While there are ethical and moral dilemmas involved in the methods discussed in this essay, we would counter the argument that certain topics should not be investigated and that families should not be subjected to the "voyeurism" of family researchers by pointing out that the research community's respect for the privacy of the family and the unwillingness to investigate certain emotional or embarrassing topics did not prevent children from being abused, did not prevent wives from being abused, did not eliminate impotence, and did not enforce the incest taboo. Nor did the perceptual blinders that family researchers wore when viewing the family prevent myths and conventional wisdoms from being accepted as fact when scientific data on sensitive topics was lacking. If we are to learn more about the basic nature of the family and family functioning, and if we are to be capable of dealing with some of the fundamental social problems that exist in the family, we must be prepared to take the risks in the study of sensitive topics and to seek creative and humane solutions to the ethical problems of such research.

NOTES

1. The author has had informed consent requirements waived in two research projects. There is no guarantee, however, that such waivers would be granted in all instances of sensitive research.

2. On May 20, 1976, United States District Judge Charles B. Renfrew of California ruled that a Harvard professor did not have to disclose information obtained confidentially in the course of academic research.

Chapter 10

ETIOLOGY OF VIOLENCE: OVERCOMING

FALLACIOUS REASONING IN UNDERSTANDING

FAMILY VIOLENCE AND CHILD ABUSE

Early child abuse researchers were physicians, psychiatrists, social workers, and other clinicians. Their work was based on at-hand cases. Control groups were rarely used. Almost uniformly, the conclusions drawn by these researchers dealt with personality and some social traits, which are said to characterize child abusers. However, lacking control groups, the researchers had no way of knowing whether the traits they felt were causally associated with child abuse were, in fact, overrepresented, underrepresented, or similarly represented in the population at large. Thus, on the basis of the early research, it was impossible to determine whether certain psychological factors were causally associated with child abuse. In fact, as I reread the early essays on child abuse, and even some of the current essays which purport to document numerous psychological traits associated with child abuse, I find profiles of my students, my neighbors, my wife, myself, and my son. It

From Richard J. Gelles, "Etiology of Violence: Overcoming Fallacious Reasoning in Understanding Family Violence and Child Abuse." Appeared in *Conference Proceedings: Child Abuse: Where Do We Go From Here?* 1978, Washington, D.C.: Children's Hospital National Medical Center.

would almost seem that some of these researchers are right when they conclude that child abusers are a random cross-section of the population. However, their research does not tell us anything. Because control groups were not used, there is absolutely no basis upon which to draw any conclusions whatsoever.

Let us look at a specific example. Suppose researchers say that 80% of their sample of child abusers have certain neurological impairments. Do they tell us what percentage of the population at large has those same neurological impairments? The Srole (1962) study of mental illness in midtown Manhattan found that as many as 80% of a randomly selected population were physically and/or psychologically impaired by psychological distress. Therefore, to say that 80% of abusers are impaired by psychological distress may in fact mean only that psychological distress is in no way specifically associated with child abusers. In the absence of control groups, many such conclusions about the causes of child abuse are not very meaningful. It has only been in the last three or four years that child abuse research has begun to consider the inclusion of randomly selected or matched control groups in study samples.

A second problem of much research to date has been the use of the medical model. This research paradigm forces a constricted and narrow focus on the study of child abuse. When attempting to explain individual cases of a phenomenon's occurrence, epidemiologists tend to look for commonalities present or factors absent in that phenomenon. An epidemiologist looking for the cause of Legionnaire's disease would examine factors that are common to people who have the disease and absent among people who do not have the disease. Medical researchers are trained to think of behavioral malfunctions or dysfunctions as being caused by one or two germs or toxins in the individual. The problem is that a paradigm of research which explains a phenomenon on the basis of one or two factors, or a combination of a few factors, tends to omit from consideration the complex series of variables and interactions of variables that are part of the causal explanation of social behavior. The medical model, the "search for the germ technique," is inappropriate to the analysis of social phenomena because it uses a biological metaphor for social behavior. Child abuse is a social phenomenon, not a biological or medical phenomenon. It cannot be studied by search for the germ techniques.

The numerous studies of violence and child abuse which have been carried out over the last 20 years are examples of the problems with the medical model explanation of child abuse. Most of these studies are capable of explaining only 4% to 5% of the variance found in the dependent variable because the research is limited to looking at only one or two causal variables. The studies do not consider patterns of variables; they do not consider time order; they do not use multiple regression techniques of analysis or pathanalysis techniques; they do not even consider interaction effects.

The extra y-chromosome argument is another example of the epidemiological approach. It was only a month ago that I heard a prominent director of a social service agency state that one of the causal factors of child abuse and violence in America is the presence of an extra y-chromosome. This individual argued that Richard Speck, the man who murdered nine nurses some years ago, possessed this extra y-chromosome. Well, it so happens Richard Speck did not have an extra y-chromosome (Shah, 1970a, 1970b). In fact by 1971, the theory of the extra y-chromosome as a viable explanation of violence had been disproven. However, an epidemiological or medical approach tends to encourage notions such as that of the extra y-chromosome because it tends to focus on one fact, one variable, one germ.

Let us look at a more positive example of the research done by sociologist Robert Sokol at Dartmouth College (1976). He found that the variables of social class and social stress were unrelated to child abuse potential, *when examined one at a time.* However, he went on to use more appropriate analytical techniques. He then found that there is a very strong interaction effect such that a combination of certain stresses found among certain people in certain social groups does, in fact, create child abuse potential. Thus, in the area of child abuse, if you look for variables as epidemiologists do—one variable at a time—you are likely to rule out class and stress as causes. The relevancy of class and stress as causal factors is clear only if the interaction effect between the two is examined.

The third problem of much child abuse research, particularly that conducted by those in the fields of medicine, psychiatry and social work, is the fallacy of false time priority. Many researchers have tended to attribute causal status to variables which may have occurred or arisen *after* the violent or abusive act. For example, abusers have been described as paranoid and depressed. This finding is typically based on an interview with a suspected parent after they have brought their child to a clinic or an emergency room. On the basis of such studies we cannot conclude that these psychological states existed before the abusive act took place. It is just as possible that being labeled a child abuser contributes to the creation of these psychological states *after* the violent incident. The same line of reasoning that argues that child abusers are paranoid and that paranoia is a cause of child abuse, would lead one to conclude that paranoia is the cause of getting speeding tickets because people who receive tickets tend to act paranoid when the police officer approaches them.

The fourth major problem of many child abuse studies is the fallacy of the search for the perfect association. This fallacious reasoning underlies the argument that because some rich people abuse their children, poverty or low-socioeconomic status cannot be a cause of child abuse. Three of the four criteria for demonstrating a causal explanation in the social sciences are: (1) that an association be demonstrated to be of a significant magnitude and a consistent pattern; (2) nonspurious; and (3) based on an established time order (that the causal factor precede the caused factor). In order to conclude that socioeconomic status or occupational prestige is a causal factor, it is not necessary to prove that *all poor people* abuse their children and that absolutely no rich people abuse their children. One must simply establish a relationship between a factor and child abuse or violence to support the claim of causality of a factor. *There need not be a perfect association.*

There are those who take the fallacy of perfect association to an even further extreme, saying that factor must explain 100% of the variance and that there may exist no other factors which can explain a phenomenon. Again, a factor does not even have to show a *major* association; it does not have to explain 90%, 80%, or even 75% of the variance. A factor need only (1) have a *significant* association; (2) have taken place before the violent or abusive act; and (3) be nonspurious.

The criterion that an association between variables be non-spurious is very important. Take for example the relationship between alcohol and violence. It is commonly held that people who drink excessively tend to be violent, and that people who drink tend to abuse their children. However, the causal relationship implied here between drink and violence tends to disappear when you investigate whether people believe they will or will not be held responsible for their actions when drunk. A story told by Murray Straus illustrates this point well. A counselor was interviewing a couple with a history of wife abuse. The counselor asked the husband, "Why do you beat up your wife?" The husband responded, "I can't control myself. I just lose control." The counselor, being a very wise person, asked, "Well, why don't you shoot her or stab her?" The husband had no response to that because the only answer he could have given would be "I can't stab or shoot my wife, I might hurt her." He knew very well what he was doing.

The research evidence shows that people *do* get drunk and beat their wives and children, but they are fully aware of what they are doing. So aware in fact, that people will drink knowing that their inebriation will give them an excuse for their violence. Thus, the commonly assumed association between alcohol and violence tends to be spurious.

The recent theory that the rising unemployment rates are associated with the rising child abuse statistics exemplifies a fifth problem, that of the "ecological fallacy." Intuitively, the notion that unemployment is causally related to child abuse makes sense, given the fact that research seems to indicate that unemployed people are more likely to abuse their children. However, it is inappropriate to interpret individual behavior on the basis of an examination of aggregate rates. The observation that both unemployment rates and child abuse rates are rising tells us nothing more than that the rates are rising simultaneously. We cannot conclude that unemployed people are abusing their children from these statistics. In fact, even if both the unemployment rates and the rate of child abuse decreased, we would not know if unemployed people who had become employed had stopped abusing their children. There are any number of plausible, if not accurate, hypotheses to explain that relationship. For instance, the simultaneous decrease in unemployment and child abuse rates may mean that hot-line volunteers have found employment, and thus, the recorded rate of child abuse has slowed down. The point is that we must question whether a statistic actually indicates something about individual behavior or whether it is simply an incidental association between rates.

The sixth problem is that our analyses of the causes of child abuse are typically based on at-hand clinical and medical cases, cases that have been officially labeled as child abuse, cases. Most of the research to date, and this includes nine of the 11 projects funded by the National Center on Child Abuse and Neglect, define child abuse in terms of the cases which are identified or caught by child protection services, state agencies, local chapters of the Society for the Prevention of Cruelty to Children, and the like. The statistics of such agencies reflect an overrepresentation of poor people, black people, marginal people, and Spanish-speaking people. The conclusion generally drawn from these statistics is that discrimination, or lack of integration into society, is somehow causally related to child abuse. This was a theory which I accepted for a long time until, through my own research, I realized that it is *possible* that the factors associated with being vulnerable to being labeled (caught) a child abuser are confounded with the factors associated with *being* a child abuser. This is a problem of such magnitude that one cannot know for certain whether poverty causes child abuse or whether poverty makes the parents vulnerable to getting caught.

Ned Polsky (1969), who studies criminal and deviant behavior, has argued for years that you cannot try to explain the causes of delinquency, deviancy, and criminal behavior by interviewing inmates in prisons. A study of such a population is a study of the unsuccessful criminals, the ones who have been caught. Similarly, it is the successful child abusers that we do not know about, those who are insulated from the official reporting system. Any explanation of the causes of child abuse must take such individuals into consideration. This means that our research can no longer take a short-cut to defining child abuse by saying that child abuse is represented by all the cases that come to the attention of the authorities. When the three-year funding period of the research projects sponsored by the National Center on Child Abuse and

Neglect ends, we are going to know a lot about who gets caught and why they get caught; but ultimately, we will probably know very little about what causes people to abuse their children. This is not to say that this kind of research presents us with no evidence at all—it does and I will present some of that evidence shortly. However, this research presents us with evidence of associations, not causal relationships. It presents possibilities of variables associated with child abuse which should not be considered as causal explanations.

The seventh problem is that causal relationships and/or conclusions tend to result from post hoc examination of data. A very well-known study is a prime example. The researchers constructed the longest interview schedule they thought was tenable, administered it, coded it, put it in a computer, and spent two and one-half years playing with the data to see what things fit together. In my opinion, that is not a test for causal relationships. It is a gold-mining operation which looks for associations and nothing more.

The eighth problem is that of an inappropriate methodological approach to the presentation of tabular data. It is a problem which has plagued even the classic researchers in the field of child abuse. Let us look at Table 1 which presents the relationship between education and child abuse (Table 1 presents data from an actual study of abuse). In this table the independent or proposed causal variable, is "education." The dependent variable, the factor which we are trying to explain, is child abuse. In order to standardize the data and interpret the table we must first percentage the raw data. There are three ways to present the percentaged data. The first, which actually reveals nothing, would be to divide the number of cases in each cell by the total number of cases in the table (N=409). Doing this, however, reveals nothing about the possible association between education and child abuse. The second approach is to percentage in the direction of the dependent variable. In Table 1a we have percentaged in the direction of the dependent variable by dividing the number of cases in each cell by the total number of cases in each category of the dependent variable. The question answered by this approach is "what percent of child abusers have 'x' amount of education?" At first glance it would appear that the most likely abusers are those with 10-12

Table 10:   Education by Child Abuse

Years of Education	Abused Child	Did Not Abuse	Total
0–6	24	11	35
7–9	42	46	88
10–12	140	104	244
some college	13	17	30
college degree	2	6	8
graduate study	2	2	4
Total	223	183	409

Table 10a: Education by Child Abuse

Years of Education	Abused Child	Did Not Abuse
0–6	11%	6%
7–9	19%	25%
10–12	63%	56%
some college	6%	9%
college degree	1%	3%
graduate study	1%	2%
Total	100%	100%

Table 10b: Education by Child Abuse

Years of Education	Abused Child	Did Not Abuse	Total
0–6	69%	31%	100%
7–9	48%	52%	100%
10–12	57%	43%	100%
some college	43%	57%	100%
college degree	25%	75%	100%
graduate study	50%	50%	100%

years of education (69% of the abusers had 10-12 years of schooling). However, this conclusion is misleading. For one, it simply presents the educational distribution of child abusers. One would expect there to be more abusers in the 10-12 years of education category, because most of the population of the United States falls into this range (the median number of years of schooling for the population is between 11 and 12).

What we need to know is not what the education of the child abuser is, but what percentage of child abusers have x years of education and what percentage of people with that level of education do not abuse their children. In other words, are people with one level of education more or less likely to abuse their children? To answer this question, one must percentage the table in the direction of the independent variable as we have done in Table 1b. From this table it can be seen that the greatest difference between abusers and nonabusers is at the lowest and highest ends of the education continuum. In other words, those with the least education are most likely to abuse, while the most educated are the least likely to abuse.

This is a very simple example, but it does demonstrate that different results can be obtained from the same data set, depending on how the data are presented in tabular form.

In the last 10 years, the issue of child abuse has become a priority; the federal government decided that child abuse was an important area; agencies decided that this was a problem they wanted to confront; and we have engaged in a headlong rush to try to understand the causes of child abuse and to solve the problem. A side-effect of this focus of attention has been a tendency to accept and repeat conclusions with little critical awareness. Questionable statistics are cited and recited until they become accepted as fact, until they are accepted as common knowledge. However, many of these statistics are a product of a kind of statistical alchemy. For an example, let us look at the national statistics on the incidence of child abuse. The only reputable figures are those presented by David Gil (1970). Too many other researchers present national statistics which are developed through projections made on the basis of the incidence of child abuse in only one area of the country. For example, Douglas Besharov, the director of the National Center of Child Abuse and Neglect, takes the reported cases from New York state and projects figures for the entire country.

As should be clear from the problems which I have presented, it is incumbent upon those in the field of child abuse to not simply repeat conclusions and associations, to not accept them as fact; but rather, to ask of every citation: What are the rules of evidence that support these conclusions? How viable are these conclusions?

In the future we need research which does not rely on caught or at-hand cases exclusively, we need to use control groups and comparison groups, and we need more studies which are based on representative samples. I think we use at-hand cases because it is convenient, we do not want to get our hands too dirty. It is dirty work to go door-to-door and try to ferret out the unreported cases. However, it is precisely those unreported cases which are going to provide us with an understanding of what causes child abuse, rather than what causes people to get caught.

I would also recommend that we do research which tests theories. To my knowledge, there are only one or two projects funded by HEW which actually propose to test a specific theory and either verify it or reject it in terms of the cause of child abuse. The majority of research projects underway are clinical gold-mining operations which hope to come up with a nugget after dredging through thousands upon thousands of responses to inappropriately lengthy interview schedules.

We also need research which has the potential to generate theories. If we cannot test theories, at least we can attempt to generate them. Too many research endeavors stop at the associational level. They present all the material I have presented today, but do not go on to say what the data means in terms of a theory of child abuse.

Finally, I recommend that we conduct our research about a phenomenon which can be operationalized. I have studied family violence because it can be measured and conceptualized. Child abuse cannot be measured and conceptualized. Child abuse is a political term which was designed to bring attention to an area where children's rights were overlooked. Child abuse is not a specific behavior which can be operationalized and tested. As long as the federal government thinks they can conduct a national incidence study of child abuse, they are doomed to failure.

Child abuse is a nice word to use if you are going to have a conference. It is a nice word to use if you want to convince somebody that you are fundable. But, once you have got the money, forget it. Choose a discrete phenomenon that can be measured and then attempt to explain specific acts of neglect, specific acts of abuse, specific acts against children. This area needs study. It has suffered too long from being overpoliticized and underresearched.

Part IV

THE IMPACT OF FAMILY VIOLENCE

Introduction

THE IMPACT OF FAMILY VIOLENCE

Most studies of violence toward children have found a relationship between being the victim of violence as a child and using violence in the home as an adult. This finding has often taken on a deterministic flavor. Much of the public, and some professionals, interpret the research to mean that *all* abused children *will* grow up to be abusive adults, and that anyone who is not abused as a child will grow up to be nonviolent.

Our own research, and our recently completed national survey of violence in the family (Straus, Gelles, and Steinmetz, 1979), supports a *probabilistic* interpretation that violence does beget violence.

Other students of violent behavior have found that the impact of violent upbringing extends outside the home. Research on murderers finds that killers experience more frequent and severe violence than their nonhomicidal brothers (Palmer, 1962; Gillen, 1946). Examinations of presidential assassins or would-be assassins also find these individuals sharing common histories of violent upbringings. In his diary, Arthur Bremer, Governor George Wallace's would-be assassin wrote, "My mother must have thought I was a canoe, she paddled me so much." Lee Harvey Oswald,

Sirhan Sirhan, and Charles Manson all experienced violent child-hoods (Button, 1973).

A survey of violent inmates in San Quentin prison found that 100% of them experienced extreme violence between the ages of one and 10 (Maurer, 1976).

Unfortunately, many of the studies used to reach the conclusion that violence in the home leads to violence in the street are flawed by many of the methodological problems mentioned in the previous essay. And while the "crucial experiment" which tests the proposition that violence at home produces violence outside the home has not, and for ethical reasons may never be conducted, we do find results from research using various samples and various methods supporting such a hypothesis.

Our own investigation of the societal impact of violence in the home was a detailed examination of research on support for the death penalty. Our research on family violence demonstrated that observing and experiencing violence raised the likelihood of later violent behavior, and Owens and Straus (1975) found a relationship between childhood experience with violence and approval of interpersonal violence. Our review of the literature on the death penalty and our own research on family violence led to the development of a theoretical framework which proposed that experiencing violence as a child increases the likelihood that an individual will support capital punishment.

The proposition that experiencing violence at home increases support for violence outside the home brings us full circle in our examination of family violence. We had begun our research with the notion that the general high level of support and approval of violence in our society, as evidenced by support for the death penalty and corporal punishment in the schools, contributed to the acceptability of violence in the home. Now we see that violence in the home may well contribute to the high levels of support for violence in the society.

Chapter 11

FAMILY EXPERIENCE AND PUBLIC SUPPORT

FOR THE DEATH PENALTY

(with Murray A. Straus)

In the *Furman* decision (Furman versus Georgia, 1972), the
Supreme Court reaffirmed its previous position that the operational definition of "cruel and unusual" changes as the standards
of society change. However, there was a high degree of disagreement among the Justices concerning the state of public opinion on
the death penalty (Vidmar and Ellsworth, 1974). It therefore
became critical to ascertain where the public really stands on the
issue of capital punishment and, as proposed by Justice Marshall,
how enlightened and informed public opinion is on the topic of
the death penalty (Furman versus Georgia, 1972). The point
Justice Marshall made was that the court should be guided only by
public opinion which evidences informed and enlightened knowledge. Thus, Vidmar and Ellsworth (1974) conclude, only to the
extent that the public is knowledgable about both the utilitarian
and humanitarian aspects of capital punishment can we rely on
public opinion to judge whether the death penalty is consistent
with "evolving standards of decency" (Trop versus Dulles, 1958).

Reprinted, with permission, from the American Journal of Orthopsychiatry. Copyright
1975 by the American Orthopsychiatric Association, Inc.

The task of establishing the extent to which public opinion is "informed and enlightened" is extremely difficult because of the many complex and interrelated factors which go into the formation of public opinion. This essay is addressed to one of these factors: the part played by early family experiences in leading people to support or oppose capital punishment.

If we are to understand fully how enlightened and informed the public is on the subject of the death penalty, it is not sufficient to assess the level of support for the death penalty, nor to list and analyze the social, political, and personality variables related to support and nonsupport. To fully address the issue raised by Justice Marshall, and to comprehend more completely the meaning of public opinion vis á vis the death penalty, we need to know something about *how* people come to support the death penalty and what kind of death penalty they favor. This is because the process of coming to support the death penalty may be characterized by bigotry, violence, and repression rather than by an open examination of the ethical and practical aspects of capital punishment. If, for the most part, it takes family processes characterized by the former rather than the latter conditions to produce individuals who favor the death penalty, this fact could be an important basis for judging the degree to which public support for the death penalty is consistent with emerging standards of decency.

This essay will attempt to answer the question by drawing on results of research from two separate but related fields of inquiry. From the research on support for the death penalty we shall draw on data and theories which portray the type of individual who supports capital punishment, and from our own work on intra-family violence we shall suggest the family processes which are likely to produce the type of person who favors the death penalty. More specifically, we will propose that there are certain family socialization antecedents which lead people to favor the use of capital punishment, and that, in practice, supporters would apply the death penalty in a way that is situationally specific to such a degree as to constitute a discriminatory application of the penalty.

Family Experiences and the Death Penalty Controversy

There are three main reasons for focusing on the relation of family experience to support for the death penalty:

(1) As previously noted, if the circumstances producing support for the death penalty are, in and of themselves, inconsistent with the emerging moral and social standards of society, this fact alone will enter the overall assessment of the degree to which the death penalty is based on enlightened and informed public opinion.

(2) If there is evidence that those who support use of the death penalty tend to base this on discriminatory application against a particular class, race, or sex, the inappropriate basis on which such support rests would open the way for the Court to rule that capital punishment is cruel and unusual (Vidmar and Ellsworth, 1974).

(3) Information on the specific process by which people come to acquire a favorable view of the death penalty will help us to understand what it means to its supporters when they express such support. For example, their belief acquisition process may be relevant to the issue of discretionary application of the death penalty and to the rash of so-called "mandatory" death penalty statutes. When 50% to 60% of the public expresses support for the death penalty, does this mean that they will, in practice, support a mandatory death penalty? By examining the processes through which a child experiences and learns about physical punitiveness, it may be possible to anticipate just how mandatory the new statutes are likely to be in practice.[1]

The approach to be followed in relating family experience to the death penalty starts in the next section with the identification of the social and psychological characteristics of those who support the death penalty. Following this, we review evidence from research on the amount and nature of violence between family members, and the consequences this has for the emerging values and personality of the child. Finally, we show the correspondence between these values and personality characteristics and the characteristics of those who favor the death penalty.

Variations in Level of Public Support

National sample surveys have yielded a consistent pattern of level of support for the death penalty. Erskine (1970) reported that support for the use of the death penalty in murder cases declined from 62% in 1936 to 42% in 1966. The trend reversed after 1966, and the level of support rose to 51% in 1969. The most recent data, from the Harris 1973 polling and the National Opinion Research Center General Social Survey of 1973, indicate that 59% of Americans *believe* in capital punishment (Harris et al., 1973) and 59% of Americans *favor* the use of capital punishment (NORC). These national sample surveys have been supplemented by regional and statewide surveys that yield essentially the same longitudinal patterns of support.

The utility of these national and statewide surveys in coming to grips with the question of how people come to support the death penalty is minimal. There are any number of plausible hypotheses concerning why the level of support for capital punishment declined for three decades and then reversed direction for the last 10 years. One line of reasoning might suggest that the public's support for the penalty diminished as the penalty was actually used, but when executions declined and finally were eliminated in the 1960s, people began to blame the rising crime rate on the elimination of the hypothetical deterrent—capital punishment. Another possible explanation is that with wide media distribution of figures on crime rates and reports of exotic violent crimes, people became more fearful of victimization—particularly from widely publicized "senseless" crimes such as the "Manson family" killings in California. This fear could have become translated into a growing desire to have a deterrent and a punishment available which would hopefully reduce violent crime and allay fears of victimization.

These theories are, of course, highly speculative, and we are inclined to believe, as sociologists, that a major part of the reason for the shift in support is not to be found on the individual level, but on the societal level. We tend to agree with Becker (1963) that cries for law and order are more the product of an "enterprise" in the form of a "moral crusade" than an articulation of society's basic values. Thus, fluctuation in support for the death penalty over time may be due to effective moral crusades by individuals, who, for a variety of reasons, advocate the use of the death penalty. A case in point is the 1974 primary campaign for attorney general in Massachusetts. One candidate's law-and-order campaign featured radio advertisements urging the death penalty as a deterrent to crime. Support for capital punishment seems to be strongly correlated with "law-and-order" campaigns by local, state, and national politicians. It is one stark means a candidate has of displaying that he will "do something about crime" if elected.

If, then, changes in national levels of support for the death penalty are possibly explainable as a result of moral crusades embodied in the political process, we need to look for hints as to how people come to accept the message of these moral crusades. This must also be dealt with at both the societal and the individual level.

At the societal level, we suggest that during periods in which the society itself is engaged in violent acts, namely during wartime, public approval of violence of all types tends to increase. This is shown in the study (Huggins and Straus, 1979) of violence in children's literature from 1850 to 1970. The bulk of violent acts depicted in stories for children were "instrumental," were successful in achieving the intended goal, and were presented in a context of social approval for the violent acts. In fact, many are implicit examples of the death penalty, such as the big bad wolf who is boiled alive for blowing the house down. That study also found that, although there was no general tendency for the number of violent incidents either to decrease or to increase over this 120-year period, there is a striking pattern of ups and downs in the average number of violent acts depicted, with the high points corresponding to the periods in which the United States was at war. Thus, in times of war—such as the Vietnam war period which coincided with the increase in public approval of the death penalty—at least one type of mass media reveals a sharp increase in content presenting *and approving* of instrumental violence closely akin to the death penalty (Huggins and Straus, 1979).

Although we do not have quantitative evidence for adult mass media, the growth in number and popularity of films of extreme violence during this period suggests a parallel development.

We suggest that a high level of violence in the society may not only produce a glorification of violence in books and films, but also make the public more receptive to the message of those who—for whatever reason—advocate the death penalty. But, not all of those living in violent times will be influenced by these processes. Consequently, we need to look at the individual social and psychological correlates of support for the death penalty.

Social and Psychological Correlates of Support

Research reveals that levels of support for the death penalty vary among various subpopulations. For example, people who tend to favor capital punishment are likely to be older, less educated, male, more wealthy, white, urban, Catholic, and more religious (Erskine, 1970; Vidmar and Ellsworth, 1974). Although some suggestive ideas could emerge from speculations on the process linking these social characteristics with support for the death penalty, in the absence of actual evidence it seems best to turn to studies of attitudinal and other intraindividual character-istics of death penalty supporters for an understanding of the meanings and motivations underlying support for the death pen-alty. In particular, two sets of data are relevant: (1) studies which deal with the characteristics we will call punitiveness, and (2) studies which examine dogmatism and authoritarianism.

PUNITIVENESS

A repeated finding in social psychological studies of the death penalty is that support for the death penalty is correlated with an individual's willingness and approval of the use of violence and punitiveness for social control. The support for tough laws, tough police, use of violence to control disorder, and severe treatment of criminals indicates an underlying acceptance of punitiveness to maintain social order. The Harris poll (1973) found that death penalty supporters also favor corporal punishment of criminals. This tough-mindedness carries over into a desire to have tough laws and tough courts (Thomas, unpublished study), and the holding of conservative legal attitudes (Crosson, 1966).

The high level of punitiveness evidenced in support for use of the ultimate punishment—the legal taking of a life—is generalized in the fact that people who believe in capital punishment also favor severe treatment of all criminals (Vidmar and Ellsworth, 1974). Blumenthal et al. (1972), in a study of the justification of violence, found an association between support for the death penalty and a favorable view of the use of violence by the police to maintain law and order. Similarly, just as those who favored the use of violence to maintain the status quo tended to favor the death penalty, those who endorsed the use of violence to bring about needed change also tended to support the death penalty. Thus, support for the death penalty is associated with support for the use of violence in a wide range of other situations. Rokeach and Vidmar (1973) found that death penalty advocates are also likely to be more punitive jurors than are those who do not advocate this penalty. Finally, a major contribution to understanding the basis for public attitude about the death penalty is the essay by Thomas and Foster (1975), which develops a sociological model to explain sources of support for the death penalty. The key variable in the Thomas and Foster model, for purposes of this essay, is the belief that punishment is an effective deterrent. They find a correlation of .84 between perceived effectiveness of punishment and willingness to support capital punishment, i.e., those people who believe in the instrumental value of punishment are more likely to be the supporters of the death penalty.

AUTHORITARIANISM

A second consistency is found in the personality attributes of death penalty supporters. Authoritarianism, dogmatism, discrimination, and respect for age all are associated with what Adorno and his colleagues (1950) labeled the "authoritarian personality."

A number of psychological studies have found that death penalty supporters are authoritarian (Jurow, 1971; Rokeach and Vidmar, 1973), dogmatic (Cuncinotta, 1969; Rokeach and McClelland, 1969-1970; Rokeach and Vidmar, 1973; Snortum and Ashear, 1972) and have a deep respect for age (Comrey and Newmeyer, 1965). Discrimination is also a correlate of support for capital punishment.

Other studies have also found death penalty supporters to be conviction-prone jurors (Jurow, 1971; Rokeach and Vidmar, 1973).

In addition to these data, individuals with authoritarian personalities are more likely to perceive members of outgroups (ethnic and religious minorities) as the main violators of the law, and consequently as the main threats to their own personal safety. Epstein's research on authoritarianism and aggression towards outgroups (1965, 1966) indicates that authoritarian individuals are more likely to be punitive towards members of perceived outgroups. Thus, in their situational and actor-specific evaluation of a crime, authoritarians are most likely to support the death penalty being used on members of outgroups.

As a result of the convergence in these data, we propose that support for the death penalty can profitably be examined by exploring those socialization antecedents that produce the personality traits and the social and political attitudes which have been found associated with support for the death penalty. To do this we shall examine the institution of the family and see how violence in the family leads to approval, and the actual use, of violence for social control in the family, and the general approval of violence outside the family.[2]

Violence in the Family and Socialization for Violence

When one wants to examine or explain violence and approval of violence, the focus is typically not on the institution of the family. The focus is more likely to be violence in the streets in the form of assault, homicide, or riots and rebellion. Attempts to explain violence typically concern nonfamilial settings and institutions such as the mass media (Larsen, 1968). By contrast, the evidence shows that the family is a major—and perhaps *the* major—social unit within which the meaning and uses of violence are learned. There are at least eight reasons for this:

(1) The family is the most frequent single locus of all types of violence ranging from slaps, to beatings, to torture, to murder (Steinmetz and Straus, 1973b; 1974; Straus, 1974a). Students of homicide are well aware that more murder victims are members of the same family than any other category of murder-victim relationship. As a specific example (Boston Globe, 1973), 31% of the 255 homicides in Atlanta in 1972 were the result of domestic quarrels. Data for the entire United States reveal that from 20% to 50% of murders take place within the family (Boudouris, 1971; Goode, 1971; Palmer, 1972; Truninger, 1971). From our own research, we estimate violent incidents between husbands and wives occur at least once in perhaps as many as 50% of American families (Gelles, 1974; Straus, 1974a). In fact, violence is so common in the family that we have said that it is at least as typical of family relations as is love.

Research on child abuse suggests that perhaps as many as 2 million children a year in the United States are victims of the form of violence called child abuse (Gil, 1971; Light, 1974). Other studies (Gelles, 1973; Gil, 1971; Steele and Pollock, 1968) reveal that child abusers are likely to have been abused as children. This is consistent with our own studies, from which we concluded that the family is a "training ground" for violence, teaching both the overt acts of violence and violence approval (Gelles, 1974; Owens and Straus, 1975).

Thus, from earliest childhood until death, a person is more likely to observe, to commit, and to be the victim of violence within the family than in any other setting. Moreover, unlike violence in other situations, the family provides a model for violence that cuts across age and sex taboos. Adults hit children in the family, but not typically elsewhere; men hit women and women hit men when they are husband and wife, but this is not often seen outside the family.

(2) Intrafamily violence, unlike violence between other persons, is likely to be legitimate in the eyes of the actors and others. This is most clearly the case with parental use of physical punishment on children, which is not merely legitimate—it is almost a normative requirement (Gelles, 1974; Steinmetz and Straus, 1974; Straus, 1974a). Stark and McEvoy (1970), using data from a national survey on violence, also found general approval for the use of force on children. This is not confined only to young children. Both Straus (1971) and Steinmetz (1974) found that half of their samples of college freshmen had been hit by their parents or threatened with being hit during their senior year in high school. Moreover, this normative approval or permissiveness of violence extends to violence between siblings and between spouses. In the case of spouses, there are contradictory norms and values that make it more difficult to perceive the extent to which acts of physical force, which would produce criminal or civil charges if they occurred between unmarried persons, are not so regarded if between husband and wife unless severe physical injury results (and often not even then).

(3) Because intrafamily violence is between those who are closest to each other in a social-psychological sense, the observation and experience of such violence by a child carries the message that even violence between intimates is both permissible and legitimate.

(4) Violence is commonly employed for moral training and character development. Many parents fear that they will spoil or harm their children if they do *not* use strict discipline (i.e., force). The message these parents convey is that children *need* to be hit.

In addition, parents believe that force is a swift and effective method of training and controlling the behavior of their children.

Parents not only believe that children *need* to be hit, many parents also believe that children *deserve* to be hit, as the following sentiments illustrate:

> Mrs. (56): Well, if they are told not to do something that they've been told over and over again that's it . . . I catch them doing it, well, they deserve a spanking.

> Mrs. (59): I spank her once a week—when she deserves it—usually when she is eating [Gelles, 1974].

The fact that many parents use physical punishment when in their view the children deserve it indicates a retributive dimension of legitimate violence in the family.

(5) Violence in the family is largely instrumental. As we have seen in the previous discussion, legitimate violence is closely linked with the use of violence in the family to achieve some goal or desired end on the part of the user. Thus, some of the husbands in Gelles's study (1974) stated that they "need" to hit their wives to calm them down (!); parents stated that they hit their children to teach them not to run into the street or to be wary of plugs and wires, or to toilet train them (1974: 58 ff).

The rational-instrumental nature of much family violence is shown by what can be called the *calculus of administration*. For many people, the thought of using violence on another person can only be seen as an act of an irrational human being. But our research reveals a pattern of strikingly rational and coherent nature. Parents who use force on their children use a defined calculus of administration:

> The feature that characterizes the normal use of violence to punish children is the elaborate calculus that parents employ for deciding what type of behavior deserves what type of punishment. There are both implicit and explicit rules for using violence that parents develop in interaction with their children that they expect their children to learn and to adhere to. The child is expected to know that if he does a certain thing he will receive a certain punishment. The parent, on the other hand, tries desperately to follow these rules and to punish the child consistently. Thus, an aspect of normal violence between parent

and child is the building of common sense understandings about rules
of conduct and rules of punishment [Gelles, 1974: 68].

Consequently, we find that legitimate-instrumental violence is
used by parents and experienced by children in a situation-actor-
specific manner which implies that each case is judged on its own
merits before the punishment is administered, and that the punishment is administered with some desired instrumental end in mind.

(6) A large number of parents feel a moral obligation to train
their children *in the use of violence*. Boys, especially, are taught to
be tough. The survey conducted for the National Commission on
the Causes and Prevention of Violence found that almost three-
quarters of their national sample felt that "when a boy is growing
up it is very important for him to have a few fist fights" (Stark
and McEvoy, 1970). In many sectors of the society it is more than
just a few, and in some, more than just fist fights (Brown, 1965).

(7) In the section of *Violence in the Family* which focuses on
"The Family as Training Ground for Societal Violence," Steinmetz and Straus (1974) distinguish between "direct training" in
violence, such as that described in the previous paragraph, and
"indirect training." The indirect training in aggression may be
more important than the direct training because it begins well
before speech and is therefore learned in such a diffuse and vague
way as to become an unconscious motive (McClelland, 1955). This
is the use of violence (i.e., spanking and slapping) as a means of
control, which typically starts in infancy. It should be no surprise
that, in addition to effecting the desired control, the child also
deeply learns that violence is an effective—even the most effective—means of dealing with others. It is something to be used
when the issue is really important.

(8) The final reason for the tremendous importance of the
family in training the next generation in the use of violence
involves the same set of factors that makes the family important
for all aspects of the child's development; such things as the early
exclusiveness or monopoly on interaction with the child, the
powerful legal and moral position of parents, and the attachment
of the child to the family.[3]

PHYSICAL PUNISHMENT AND THE RATIONAL USE OF VIOLENCE

While each of the above factors is a part of the overall pattern, the element which is of most direct relevance for understanding the role of the family in support for the death penalty is the use of physical punishment. As Bandura (1973) noted, parents who use physical punishment provide their children with an aggressive model for imitation, and they effectively teach children patterns of counteraggression. The importance of this learning situation is elaborated by Singer (1971):

> In new situations where a child is at a loss for what to do he is likely to remember what he saw his parents do and behave accordingly.... Indeed, adults when they become parents and are faced with the novelty of the role revert to the type behavior they saw their parents engage in when they were children sometimes against their current adult judgement [1971: 31].

In addition to providing models which can be imitated, families, through their use of violence, teach that violence is an acceptable form of expression or problem-solving. Owens and Straus (1975) found that experience with violence as a child (either as observer, aggressor, or victim) is correlated with approval of violence as an adult.

This normative training in the rational-instrumental use of violence is one of the two central findings in the family violence research that is applicable to support for the death penalty. The family not only trains its members to accept violence, it also trains them to accept the particular modes of violence prevalent in the family—legitimate, instrumental, situationally administered, and infused with moral indignation (Ranulf, 1964).

We argue that the process by which people come to support the death penalty begins in the family, where children are taught that: (1) violence is an effective punishing agent; (2) violence is an *acceptable* punishing agent; (3) the administration of violence is *contingent* on the particular aspects of the situation; and (4) violence may therefore be used to achieve socially approved and desired ends or goals, but its use requires discretionary judgment.

Socialization for Dogmatism and Authoritarianism

It will be recalled from the review of social and psychological correlates of support for the death penalty that individuals favoring capital punishment tend to be high in authoritarianism and dogmatism. This correlation points the way toward the second major process by which the family plays a part in accounting for public support of the death penalty, because the family experiences of a growing child are important influences on the extent to which the child will acquire the characteristics of the authoritarian-dogmatic pattern of personality.

Research on the authoritarian personality and its familial antecedents covers a 30-year period. Consequently, it will not take as long to document this relationship as was needed to document the involvement of the family in training the next generation in the meaning and use of violence. Specifically, since the original investigation by Adorno et al., studies have consistently found that authoritarian attitudes are related to severe parental punishment (Adorno et al., 1950; Epstein, 1966; Roberts and Jessor, 1958; Weatherly, 1963), including studies which control for confounding with socioeconomic status (Kaufman, 1957; Roberts and Rokeach, 1956; Smith and Rosen, 1958). The cumulative weight of these and other similar studies indicates that the authoritarian personality structure is an intervening variable which links experience with instrumental physical force in the family with support for the death penalty. The family is therefore a key part of the process producing two of the main correlates of support for the death penalty: (1) the punitive-retributive justice value system discussed in the previous section, and (2) the authoritarian-dogmatic personality discussed in this section.

In addition, the combination of these two traits takes on a greater importance than either of them alone. The same processes which tend to produce approval of violence as a legitimate means for achieving socially desirable ends (i.e., use of physical punishment in a context of legitimacy and moral correctness), also tend to produce a personality structure that negates the inflow of information which might argue against the deterrent value of violence. Dogmatic personality is characterized by rigidity of thinking, and this rigidity makes dogmatic individuals less likely to accept information that challenges their belief in the instrumental value of punishment. Thus, the socialization antecedents that lead an individual to accept and support violent punishment also produce a personality that locks him into this line of reasoning despite any contrary evidence.

Discretionary Punishment in Family and Legal Systems

If part of the process by which people come to support the death penalty is the observing and experiencing of violence by and from their parents and siblings, from which they learn approval of instrumental violence, then we can make some inferences about the type of death penalty that would be advocated and deployed by its supporters. Our research on family violence found that parents use instrumental force on their children in a situation-specific, actor-specific manner. The calculus developed by the parents includes a list of transgressions, appropriate punishments, circumstances under which the punishment should and can be administered, and a subjective construction of the appropriate reaction of the child when punished. Although parents often subscribe to an "eye for an eye" punishment (one father stated that sassing deserved a slap in the mouth because that is where the misbehavior came from), they also administer the punishment on the basis of the "goodness" or "badness" of the child and on the basis of whether the particular situation justifies the punishment. In other words, the same misbehavior is not always punished in the same way for different children or even for the same child. The administration of punishment is dependent on the subjective assessment by the parent of the particular circumstances surrounding the misbehavior and of the characteristics of a particular child.

If this is the way punishment is administered in the family, it suggests that these parents and their children who are being socialized to use force under these conditions and to approve of instrumental force in general, would not be likely to support a mandatory death penalty. It is likely that, as prosecutors, judges, jurors, or even the public at large, those whose support of the death penalty is based on this type of family experience would want to analyze the entire case before deciding what is the appropriate punishment. This inference is partially supported by the Harris survey, which found fewer people who support mandatory application of the death penalty than support the general principle of the death penalty. In addition, as pointed out in the section on authoritarianism, the discretion is likely to mean more frequent application of the death penalty to members of minority groups.

A Model for the Process Producing Social Support for the Death Penalty

In the course of this article a number of interrelated issues have been dealt with. But the style of presentation, although necessary to communicate each distinct part of the analysis, is not well suited to bring the various parts together into an overall theory or model of the process by which the family plays a key role in social support for the death penalty. The present section seeks to provide the needed integration and overview by two devices. In the first portion of the section we use deductive logic to formulate new propositions which explain how violence in the family can lead to support for the death penalty. In the second part we present a diagrammatic summary of the key variables and their relation to support of the death penalty.

PROPOSITIONAL DEDUCTIONS

Our use of deductive logic resulted in the formulation of five propositions concerning the role played by the family in molding support for the death penalty. There are three steps involved in each such derivation. First, we state a proposition that summarizes one aspect of what was presented in this essay on the meaning and use of violence in the family. These will be labeled as propositions F1, F2, and the like. Second, we state a proposition to summarize what is known about one of the social-psychological factors associated with support for the death penalty and label these D1, D2, and the like. These propositions will be presented in pairs, for example, F1 with D1. The propositions in each pair were selected and juxtaposed because they have a variable in common. Specifically, in each pair, the variable associated with advocacy of the death penalty is also the variable which is associated with intrafamily violence. The third step presents the results of this syllogism in the form of a new proposition, which explicitly sets forth the contribution that family experience makes to public support of the death penalty.

(I) An initial conclusion from our review of family violence can be summarized as *Proposition F1: The more violence is present in the family, the more likely is a person reared in that context to accept the normalcy and probable occurrence of all types of violence.* Because the typical citizen is more likely to experience or commit violent acts within the family than in any other setting or relationship, it follows that, *F2: The family is a primary place in which both approval of violence and fear of victimization is learned.* The corresponding proposition from research on the so-cial-psychological correlates of support for the death penalty is, *D1: The more one regards violence as a part of everyday life, the greater the support for the death penalty.*

> *Therefore:* To the extent that family experience is a major element in learning that force and violence are a normal part of human social life, and to the extent that regarding violence as normal is related to support for the death penalty, it can be concluded that family experiences are a major part of the causal sequence accounting for public support of the death penalty.

(II) The second deduction also starts with family propositions F1 and F2. The corresponding proposition from research on the death penalty is *D2: The greater the fear of being a victim of violence, the greater the support for the death penalty.*

> *Therefore:* To the extent that violent acts towards or by one's spouse, children, and parents is a major way in which one learns to fear the consequences of being a victim of violence, and to the extent that fear of being a victim of violence is associated with support for the death penalty, it can be concluded that family experience plays an important role in public support for the death penalty.

(III) Our review on family violence indicates that intrafamily violence is predominantly rational-instrumental and morally toned, and we concluded that, *F3: The more violence in the form of physical punishment is used by parents on their children, and the more it is used by husbands and wives as a means of securing some end, the greater the likelihood that the meaning and use of violence will be defined in rational-instrumental terms and be infused with moral indignation and rectitude.* Because we have previously shown that intrafamily violence is predominantly rational-instrumental and morally toned, it follows that *the family is a major locus for learning about the utility and moral correctness of violence.* The parallel proposition from death penalty studies is *D3: The greater the belief in the efficiency and moral correctness of punishment as a means of securing worthy ends, the greater the support for the death penalty.*

> *Therefore:* To the extent that the family is the main context in which the use of punishment and physical force is experienced and given meaning as a rational, instrumental, and morally justified act, and to the extent that this definition and evaluation of punitiveness is related to support for the death penalty, it can be concluded that the learning about punishment and violence in the family context is a main part of the causal sequence leading to support for the death penalty.

(IV) Our analysis of parent-child violence concluded that this type of intrafamily violence is not only rational-instrumental, but that it is also typically administered in a discretionary manner (e.g., what we called "the calculus of punishment"). We can summarize this in proposition *F4: The more offenses within the family are punished in proportion to the severity of the offense and in relation to the circumstances and characteristics of the offender, the more likely is the person to believe that all offenses should be dealt with according to the principles of retribution tempered by discretion in relation to the circumstances, the offense, and the character of the offender.* Studies of supporters of the death penalty find that, *D4: The greater the belief in retribution and in the idea that punishment should depend on the circumstances, motives, and characteristics of the offender, the greater the likelihood of favoring the death penalty for the gravest crimes.*

> *Therefore:* Because support for the death penalty is associated with the belief that the more severe the crime the more severe should be the punishment, taking into account the characteristics of the offender, and because belief in such a system of justice is largely learned within the family context, it follows that the near universality of family experience with this type of retributive and person-specific punishment is one

of the reasons for the wide public support of the death penalty and for the discretionary way in which it is applied.

(V) Our last proposition from research on family violence is *F6: The more punishment is used—especially physical punishment—the more likely the child is to develop a dogmatic and authoritarian personality.* And, from research on the social-psychological correlates of support for the death penalty, *D5: The greater the dogmatism and authoritarianism, the greater the support for the death penalty.*

> *Therefore:* Because punitive child rearing methods are associated with the very personality factors that are, in turn, associated with support for the death penalty, it can be concluded that the high level of punitiveness typically experienced by children in the family is a part of the explanation for the high level of public support for the death penalty.[4]

What confidence can one have in the validity of the conclusions arrived at by deductive reasoning of this type? First, it should be noted that the relationships contained in the propositions about violence in the family and about the social psychological correlates of the death penalty are stochastic rather than invariant relationships. Therefore, the derived propositions do not have the status of logical proof (Costner and Leik, 1964). They do, however, bring to light plausible links between family patterns and support for the death penalty which might not otherwise have been perceived. Moreover, the plausibility of these deductions is enhanced by the fact that some empirical work has been done on one of these derived propositions—that which asserts (III) that the type of experience with punishment which occurs in the family is part of the causal sequence leading to support for the death penalty. There are two studies of this issue. Snortum and Ashear (1972) found that, of all the items used, the best predictor for punitiveness toward first degree murderers was "What young people need most of all is strong discipline by their parents" ($r = .49$). Starr and Cutler (1972) studied actual physical punishment experienced by their respondents and found that for the men (but not the women) there was less opposition to the death penalty among those whose parents usually or always used physical punishment.

Each of these studies has its limitations, so that additional research is needed. But the fact that the available evidence is consistent with the corresponding derived proposition increases confidence in the probable validity of the entire set of derived propositions.[5]

DIAGRAMMATIC MODEL

A second way of integrating, summarizing, and gaining an overview of the materials presented in this essay concerning the process by which the public comes to favor the use of capital punishment, is presented in Figure 2. This diagram overlaps the propositional-deductive summary but it differs in the style of presentation and in what is covered. First, it does not provide the detail concerning the specific ways in which typical family experiences constitute part of the etiology of support for the death penalty. Second, it goes beyond the propositional-deductive sum-

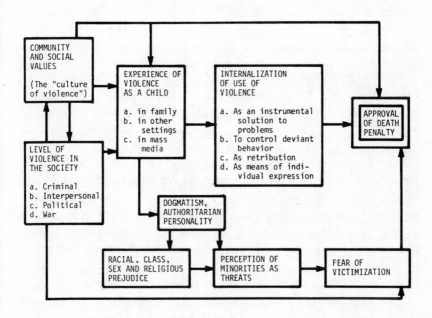

Figure 2: A Model of the Process Producing Support for the Death Penalty

mary in two ways: (1) the family is placed in context as only one of the social settings which provide the public with its experience with violence, and which define and give meaning to violence; and (2) some of the societal factors which influence the nature and frequency of intrafamily violence are shown in the boxes at the far left of the diagram.[6]

Both the propositional and the diagrammatic model are anchored in research on intrafamily violence, personality development, and the social and psychological correlates of support for the death penalty. The fact that each part is based on the results of empirical research gives us confidence in the validity of the model as a whole. However, because it is presented for the first time in this essay, it is obvious that the model as a whole has not as yet been empirically tested. It is presented as a convenient means of summarizing the way in which we have pieced together a diverse set of findings, as a means of stating our conclusions in a way which is most likely to be empirically testable, and as a stimulus for further empirical analysis and theoretical refinement.[7]

Summary and Conclusions

In this essay we have attempted to deal with the question of the extent to which public support for the death penalty is based on informed and enlightened considerations and the extent to which such support is consistent with "contemporary standards of morality." These are critical issues in respect to any future Supreme Court decision on the death penalty because three out of five Americans are reported as favoring the death penalty. Irrespective of their personal preferences, the justices of the Supreme Court are not likely to ignore such a clear majority unless it can be shown that the public view is based on standards or reflects conditions which the Court would be reluctant to accept or encourage. Our analysis suggests that support for the death penalty rests on precisely these types of unacceptable grounds.

The first step in the analytical procedure which led to this conclusion was to establish the attitude, value, and personality constellation which social-psychological research has shown to be associated with support of the death penalty. Review of these studies revealed that favorableness toward the death penalty is associated with authoritarianism and dogmatism; racial, religious, and sex prejudice; punitiveness; and acceptance of violence as a normal and morally justified part of social life. On this basis alone, one can question the extent to which support for the death penalty can be characterized as consistent with contemporary standards of morality and indicative of informed and enlightened opinion.

The second step in the analysis was to examine research on family patterns which could produce the configuration of factors just listed. It was found that certain aspects of family relationships are associated with this configuration. Specifically: (1) A high level of all types of force and violence was found to be common in families, giving rise to acceptance of violence as a normal part of life. (2) Intrafamily violence tends to be instrumental, and infused with moral indignation and rectitude, giving violence the meaning of "usefulness" and "moral correctness." (3) Intrafamily violence and punishment is used in a discretionary fashion depending on the specific circumstances and on the judgment of the goodness or badness of the person being attacked or punished, all of which are incompatible with the idea of a uniform, impersonal mandatory death sentence for specified crimes. (4) The experience of punitive child rearing—especially physical punishment—which is almost universal in American society, gives rise to punitive values, belief in retribution, and authoritarianism and dogmatism.

Overall, the analysis presented in this essay of the attitude, value and personality factors associated with public support for the death penalty, combined with the analysis which shows that the family patterns which underlie these attitudes, values and personality are marked by violence, bigotry, and repression, together lead to the conclusion that the process by which a large segment of the public comes to support the death penalty is a far cry from "informed and enlightened public opinion" or evolving standards of decency. In addition, because there seems to be little or no support, either in the family or in society, for mandatory punishment based on the infraction alone, the discretionary and erratic manner in which force and punishment is used in the family is likely to be translated into highly discriminatory application of capital punishment in society.

NOTES

1. The importance of this issue is illustrated by a recent Harris poll (1973). This national survey found a major discrepancy between general levels of support for the death penalty and people's willingness to support a specific application of the penalty. While 50% of those polled believed in the death penalty, no more than 39% could say, "If guilt were proven, I could always vote guilty even though the defendant would automatically receive the death penalty" (Harris et al., 1973). Clearly, the simple statement that one supports the death penalty is not the same as employing it when called for by law.

2. At this juncture it is necessary to point out that our working definition of violence, the nonaccidental use of physical force by one individual on another to cause injury or pain (Straus et al., 1973), would be consistent when applied to the death penalty. In other words, the death penalty will be considered violent behavior because it is the nonaccidental use of physical force to cause injury to another person.

3. This final consideration, however, should help us to avoid falling into the trap of familistic determinism in relation to violence. Just as in many other aspects of life, the influence of parents is powerful but by no means decisive. Parents have always despaired over the frequency with which they have failed to mold the child in desired directions. In the case of violence, many will take hope from this same fact.

4. Although these derived propositions center on the learning experience of children in the family, similar propositions could be formulated for the parents. That is, husbands and wives using physical punishment are also learning or reinforcing more general principles about the efficacy and moral correctness of violence for socially desirable ends. Parents learn both roles and motivations from their experience with children, just as children learn from their experience with parents.

5. Although the evidence indicates that a repressive and physically punitive set of childhood family experiences is associated with advocacy of the death penalty, at least two factors must be kept in mind in evaluating the import of this conclusion. First, "repressive and punitive" is not the opposite of permissive. Parents can use many ways to control and shape the behavior of their children in accordance with their own and society's standards of appropriate behavior with minimal or no emphasis on punishment—especially harsh physical punishment. In fact, the available evidence suggests that parental styles emphasizing punishment tend to be the least effective in respect to the child's accepting the parents' moral and ethical standards (Becker W., 1964; Hoffman, 1970). Second, the research findings on which we draw are in the form of correlations. These indicate the *degree* to which a given factor is associated with support for the death penalty; they do not indicate a necessary or sufficient relationship. Thus, for example, these data do not suggest that all who advocate the death penalty were subject to much physical punishment as children and, as adults, are dogmatic or authoritarian. There are many other factors that enter the situation to produce support for the death penalty or to undermine tendencies to favor the death penalty. In short, what we are asserting is simply that the factors discussed in this essay (and summarized in Figure 2) are indeed part of the explanation, although by no means the whole explanation.

6. For clarity in presentation, we have deliberately restricted the model presented in Figure 2 in several ways: (a) It is restricted to those variables which are analyzed in the article. (b) It omits both positive feedback loops, such as the part which experiencing violence as a child plays in creating the culture of violence, as shown in Owens and Straus (1975). (c) It is a "correlational model" and therefore does not indicate such things as contingent conditions, branching points, critical thresholds, and cybernetic

processes by which actions are monitored and controlled in relation to system goals; *see* Straus (1973) for example of a cybernetic system model of intrafamily violence.

7. Research based on either the propositional deductions or the diagrammatic model can take many forms, starting with reanalysis of existing data such as the NORC General Social Survey or the data collected for the Media Task Force of the National Commission on the Causes and Prevention of Violence. We suggest that a "synthetic longitudinal" developmental study is a type of research design likely to give a high return in relation to the time and effort expended. Such a research would investigate developmental trends in attitudes toward the death penalty by obtaining data from children at specified ages, for example, by study of those in grades 1, 3, 6, 9, and 12, and from a sample of adults at 2 different ages—perhaps 25 and 40. It would investigate such things as the age at which the concept of a death penalty is first understood by a child and if support for the death penalty varies over the life cycle thereafter. Many social-psychological phenomena show clear increases or decreases at certain ages. This design will permit identification of such turning points, which in turn, is likely to suggest something about the nature of the child's experience at that point which could account for the increase or decrease in the percentage favoring capital punishment. If it turns out that support for the death penalty is low before a certain age and high thereafter, then those interested in abolition of the death penalty will have information on a likely critical age group on which to focus some of their efforts. For this to have maximum utility, the study should not only gather information on support or opposition to the death penalty but also on the *meaning* of the death penalty to the children studied, the types of crimes for which they favor execution, and the like. If a synthetic longitudinal design of the type suggested is employed, it would be important to sample enough children at each age to permit correlational analysis designed to test the linkages shown in Figure 2 *within* age groups. This is necessary to avoid confounding the correlations with age. In addition, comparison of the pattern of correlations found at each age is likely to yield important information and insights.

CASES

FURMAN v. GEORGIA (1972) 408 U.S. 238
TROP v. DULLES (1958) 356 U.S. 86.

REFERENCES

ADORNO, T. et al. (1950) The Authoritarian Personality: Studies in Prejudice. New York: Harper & Row.

ALEXANDER, T. (1952) "The adult-child interaction test: a projective test for use in research." Monographs in Social Research and Child Development 17 (2): Serial 55.

ALLEN, C. and M. STRAUS (1975) "Resources, power, and husband-wife violence." Presented to the National Council on Family Relations in Salt Lake City.

American Humane Association (1974) "Highlights of the 1974 national data." Denver: American Humane Association. (mimeo)

AMIR, M. (1971) Patterns of Forcible Rape. Urbana, IL: University of Chicago Press.

ARIES, P. (1962) Centuries of Childhood. New York: Knopf.

BAKAN, D. (1971) Slaughter of the Innocents: A Study of the Battered Child Phenomenon. Boston: Beacon.

BANDURA, A. (1973) Aggression: A Social Learning Analysis. Englewood Cliffs, NJ: Prentice-Hall.

BARD, M. (1969) "Family intervention police teams as a community mental health resource." The Journal of Criminal Law, Criminology, and Police Science 60 (2): 247-250.

––– and B. BERKOWITZ (1969) "Family disturbance as a police function." in S. Cohen (ed.) Law Enforcement Science and Technology II. Chicago: I.I.T. Research Institute.

––– and J. ZACKER (1971) "The prevention of family violence: dilemmas of community intervention." Journal of Marriage and the Family 33 (4): 677-682.

BART, P. (1975) "Rape doesn't end with a kiss." Viva 39-42 (June): 100-102.

BECKER, H. (1963) Outsiders: Studies in the Sociology of Deviance. New York: Free Press.

––– [ed.] (1964) Perspectives on Deviance—The Other Side. New York: Free Press.

BECKER, W. (1964) "Consequences of different kinds of parental discipline," pp. 169-208 in M. Hoffman and L. Hoffman (eds.) Review of Child Development Research. New York: Russell Sage Foundation.

BEDAU, H. [ed.] (1967) The Death Penalty in Modern America. Chicago: Aldine.

BEDAU, H. and E. CURRIE (1973) "Social science research and the death penalty in America: an interim report to the Russell Sage Foundation." (mimeo)

BENNIE, E. and A. SCLARE (1969) "The battered child syndrome." American Journal of Psychiatry 125 (7): 975-979.

BERARDO, F. (1976) "Beyond the college student: an editorial comment." Journal of Marriage and the Family 38 (May): 211.

BERGER, P. and H. KELLNER (1964) "Marriage and construction of reality." Diogenes 46: 1-25.

BILLINGSLEY, A. and J. GIOVANNONI (1972) Children of the Storm. New York: Harcourt.

BLUM, F. (1970) "Getting individuals to give information to the outsider," pp. 83-90 in W. Filstead (ed.) Qualitative Methodology: Firsthand Involvement with the Social World. Chicago: Markham.

BLUM, G. (1949) "A study of the psychoanalytic theory of psychosexual development." Genetic Psychology Monographs 39: 3-99.

BLUMBERG, M. (1964) "When parents hit out." Twentieth Century 173 (Winter): 39-44.

BLUMENTHAL, M. et al. (1972) Justifying Violence: Attitudes of American Men. Ann Arbor: University of Michigan Institute for Social Research.

BOHANNAN, P. (1960) African Homicide and Suicide. New York: Athenium.

BOSSARD, J. and E. BOLL (1966) The Sociology of Child Development. New York: Harper & Row.

Boston Globe (1973) "Home strife number one cause of murders in Atlanta." February 6: 12.

BOUDOURIS, J. (1971) "Homicide and the family." Journal of Marriage and the Family 33 (November): 667-682.

BRONFENBRENNER, U. (1958) "Socialization and social class throughout time and space," pp. 400-425 in E. Maccoby, T. Newcomb, and E. Hartley (eds.) Readings in Social Psychology. New York: Holt, Rinehart & Winston.

――― (1974) "The origins of alienation." Scientific American 231: 253.

BROWN, C. (1965) Manchild in the Promised Land. New York: Macmillan.

BROWNMILLER, S. (1975) Against Our Will: Men, Women and Rape. New York: Simon and Shuster.

BULCROFT, R. and M. STRAUS (1975) "Validity of husband, wife, and child reports of conjugal violence and power." Presented to the National Council on Family Relations in Salt Lake City.

BULLARD, D. et al. (1967) "Failure to thrive in the neglected child." American Journal of Orthopsychiatry 37 (July): 680-689.

BUTTON, A. (1973) "Some antecedents of felonious and delinquent behavior." Journal of Clinical Child Psychology 2 (Fall): 35-38.

CAFFEY, J. (1946) "Multiple fractures in the long bones of infants suffering from chronic subdural hematoma." American Journal of Roentgenology, Radium Therapy, and Nuclear Medicine 58: 163-173.

――― (1957) "Some traumatic lesions in growing bones other than fractures and dislocations." British Journal of Radiology 23: 225-238.

CALVERT, R. (1974) "Criminal and civil liability in husband-wife assaults," pp. 88-90 in S. Steinmetz and M. Straus (eds.) Violence in the Family. New York: Harper & Row.

CAMPBELL D. and C. STANLEY (1963) Experimental and Quasi-Experimental Designs for Research. Chicago: Rand McNally.

CAPLOW, T. (1964) Sociology of Work. New York: McGraw-Hill.

CENTERS, R. (1949) "Marital selection and occupational strata." American Journal of Sociology 54 (May): 530-535.

COHEN, S. and A. SUSSMAN (1975) "The incidence of child abuse in the United States." (unpublished)

COLES, R. (1964) "Terror-struck children." New Republic 150 (May 30): 11-13.

COLMAN, A. and L. COLMAN. (1973) Pregnancy: The Psychological Experience. New York: Seabury.

COMREY, A. and J. NEWMEYER (1965) "Measurement of radicalism and conservatism." Journal of Social Psychology 67: 357-369.

CONGDON, T. (1970) "What goes on in his head when you're pregnant?" Glamour (December): 102ff.

COSTNER, H. and R. LEIK (1964) "Deductions from 'axiomatic theory.'" American Sociological Review 29 (December): 819-835.

CRONAN, S. (1969) Marriage. New York: The Feminist Press.

CROSSON, R. (1966) "An investigation into certain personality variables among capital trial jurors." Ph.D. dissertation, Cleveland: Case Western Reserve University.

CUMMINGS, J. (1952) "Family pictures: a projective test for children." British Journal of Psychology 43: 53-60.

CUNCINOTTA, S. (1969) "Witherspoon—will the due process clause further regulate the imposition of the death penalty?" Duquesne Law Review 7: 414-445.

CURTIS, L. (1974) Criminal Violence: National Patterns and Behavior. Lexington, MA.: Lexington Books.

DAVIDSON, T. (1978) Conjugal Crime: Understanding and Changing the Wifebeating Pattern. New York: Hawthorn Books.

DAVIS, A. (1970) "Sexual assaults in the Philadelphia prison system," pp. 107-124 in J. Gagnon and W. Simon (eds.) The Sexual Scene. Chicago: Aldine.

DAVIS, J. (1973) National Data Program for the Social Sciences. Conducted by National Opinion Research Center. Distributed by Roper Public Opinion Research Center.

DECOURCY, P. and J. DECOURCY (1973) A Silent Tragedy. New York: Alfred.

DEFRANCIS, V. and C. LUCHT (1974) Child Abuse Legislation in the 1970s. Denver: American Humane Association.

DE MAUSE, L. [ed.] (1974) The History of Childhood. New York: Psychohistory Press.
––– (1975) "Our forebearers made childhood a nightmare." Psychology Today 8 (April): 85-87.

DEXTER, L. (1958) "A note on selective inattention in social science." Social Problems 6 (Fall): 176-182.

DRAPKIN, I and E. VIANO [eds.] (1974) Victomology. Lexington, MA: Lexington Books.

DUNHAM, H. (1964) "Anomie and mental disorder," pp. 128-157 in M. Clinard (ed.) Anomie and Deviant Behavior. New York: Free Press.

DYER, E. (1963) "Parenthood as crisis: a re-study." Marriage and Family Living 25 (May): 196-201.

ECKLUND, B. (1968) "Theories of mate selection." Eugenics Quarterly 15 (June): 71-84.

ELMER, E. (1967) Children in Jeopardy: A Study of Abused Minors and Their Families. Pittsburgh: University of Pittsburgh Press.

EPSTEIN, R. (1965) "Authoritarianism, displaced aggression, and social status of the target." Journal of Personality and Social Psychology 2 (4): 585-589.
––– (1966) "Aggression toward out-groups as a function of authoritarianism and imitation of aggressive models." Journal of Personality and Social Psychology 3 (5): 574-579.

ERICKSON, K. (1962) "Notes on the sociology of deviance." Social Problems 9 (Spring): 307-314.

ERLANGER, H. (1974) "Social class and corporal punishment in childrearing: a reassessment." American Sociological Review 39 (February): 68-85.

ERSKINE, H. (1970) "The polls: capital punishment." Public Opinion Quarterly 34 (2): 290-307.

FARBEROW, N. [ed.] (1966) Taboo Topics. New York: Atherton Press.

FAULK, M. (1977) "Sexual factors in marital violence." Medical Aspects of Human Sexuality 11 (October): 30-38.

FIDLER, D. and R. KLEINKNECHT (1977) "Randomized response versus direct questioning: two data-collection methods for sensitive information." Psychological Bulletin 84 (5): 1045-1049.

FIELD, M. and H. FIELD (1973) "Marital violence and the criminal process: Neither justice nor peace." Social Service Review 47 (2): 221-240.

FONTANA, V. (1971) The Maltreated Child: The Maltreatment Syndrome in Children. Springfield, Il: Charles C. Thomas.

––– (1973) Somewhere a Child is Crying: Maltreatment–Causes and Prevention. New York: Macmillan.

FREIDSON, E. (1960) "Client control and medical practice." American Journal of Sociology 65 (January): 374-382.

FRIEDRICH W. and J. BORISKIN (1976) "The role of the child in abuse: a review of literature." American Journal of Orthopsychiatry 46 (4): 580-590.

GALDSTON, R. (1965) "Observations of children who have been physically abused by their parents." American Journal of Psychiatry 122 (4): 440-443.

––– (1975) "Preventing abuse of little children: the parent's center project for the study and prevention of child abuse." American Journal of Orthopsychiatry 45 (April): 372-381.

GALLEN, R. (1967) Wives' Legal Rights. New York: Dell.

GELLES, R. (1973) "Child abuse as psychopathology: a sociological critique and reformulation." American Journal of Orthopsychiatry 43 (July): 611-621.

––– (1974) The Violent Home: A Study of Physical Aggression Between Husbands and Wives. Beverly Hills: Sage.

––– (1975a) "On the association of sex and violence in the fantasy production of college students." Suicide 5 (Summer): 78-85.

––– (1975b) "The social construction of child abuse." American Journal of Orthopsychiatry 45 (April): 363-371.

––– (1975c) "Violence and pregnancy: a note on the extent of the problem and needed services." The Family Coordinator 24 (January): 81-86.

––– (1976) "Abused wives: why do they stay?" Journal of Marriage and the Family 38 (November): 659-668.

––– (1977) "Power, sex, and violence: the case of marital rape." Family Coordinator 26 (October): 339-347.

––– (1978a) "Methods for studying sensitive family topics." American Journal of Orthopsychiatry 48 (3): 408-424.

––– (1978b) "Violence towards children in the United States." American Journal of Orthopsychiatry 48 (October): 580-592.

––– and M. STRAUS (1979) "Determinants of violence in the family: Toward a theoretical integration," pp. 549-581 in W. Burr et al. (eds.) Contemporary Theories About the Family, vol. 1. New York: Free Press.

GIL, D. (1970) Violence Against Children: Physical Child Abuse in the United States. Cambridge, MA.: Harvard University Press.

––– (1971) "Violence against children." Journal of Marriage and the Family 33 (November): 637-648.

––– (1975) "Unraveling child abuse." American Journal of Orthopsychiatry 45 (April): 364-358.

GILLEN, J. (1946) The Wisconsin Prisoner: Studies in Crimogenesis. Madison: University of Wisconsin Press.

GILLESPIE, D. (1971) "Who has the power? The marital struggle." Journal of Marriage and the Family 33 (August): 445-458.

GIOVANNONI, J. (1971) "Parental mistreatment: perpetrators and victims." Journal of Marriage and the Family 33 (November): 649-657.

GOFFMAN, E. (1961) Asylums. New York: Anchor Books.

——— (1963) Stigma: Notes on the Management of Spoiled Identity. Englewood Cliffs, NJ: Prentice-Hall.

GOODE, E. (1969) "Multiple drug use among marijuana smokers." Social Problems 17 (Summer): 48-64.

GOODE, W. (1971) "Force and violence in the family." Journal of Marriage and the Family 33 (November): 624-636.

GRIFFEN, S. (1971) "Rape: the all-American crime." Ramparts (September): 26-35.

GUTTMACHER, M. (1960) The Mind of the Murderer. New York: Farrar, Straus, and Cudahy.

HAKEEM, M. (1957) "A critique of the psychiatric approach to the prevention of juvenile delinquency." Social Problems 5 (Fall): 194-206.

HARRIS, L. et al. (1973) "National survey on capital punishment." (unpublished)

HAWORTH, M. (1966) The CAT: Facts and Fantasy. New York: Grune and Stratton.

HEINS, M. (1969) "Child abuse—analysis of a current epidemic." Michigan Medicine 68 (17): 887-891.

HELFER, R. and C. KEMPE [eds.] (1968) The Battered Child. Chicago: University of Chicago Press.

——— (1972) Helping the Battered Child and His Family. Philadelphia: Lippincott.

HENRY, J. (1971) Pathways to Madness. New York: Vintage.

HENTIG, H. von (1948) The Criminal and His Victim: Studies in the Sociology of Crime. New Haven: Yale University Press.

HINTON, C. and J. STERLING (1975) "Volunteers serve as an adjunct to treatment for child-abusing families." Hospital and Community Psychiatry 26 (March): 136-137.

HOBBS, D. (1965) "Parenthood as crisis: a third study." Journal of Marriage and the Family 27 (August): 367-372.

HOFFMAN, M. (1970) "Moral development," pp. 261-360 in P. Mussen (ed.) Carmichael's Manual of Child Psychology, II. New York: John Wiley.

HOLLINGSHEAD, A. (1950) "Cultural factors in the selection of mates." American Sociological Review 15 (October): 619-627.

HOOKER, E. (1966) "Male homosexuality," pp. 44-55 in N. Farberow (ed.) Taboo Topics. New York: Atherton Press.

HOROWITZ, I. and M. LIEBOWITZ (1967) "Social deviance and political marginality: toward a redefinition of the relation between sociology and politics." Social Problems 15: 280-296.

HORVITZ, D., B. GREENBERG, and J. ABERNATHY (1975) "Recent developments in randomized response designs," pp. 271-285 in J. Srivastava (ed.) A Survey of Statistical Design and Linear Models. New York: American Elsevier.

HUERTA, F. (1976) "Incest: the neglected form of child abuse." Presented to the Western Social Science Association in Phoenix, Arizona.

HUGGINS, M. and M. STRAUS (1979) "Violence and the social structure as reflected in children's books from 1850-1970," in M. Straus and G. Hotaling (eds.) The Social Causes of Husband-Wife Violence. Minneapolis, MN: University of Minnesota Press.

HUMPHREYS, L. (1970) Tearoom Trade: Impersonal Sex in Public Places. Chicago: Aldine.

HUNT, M. (1973) "Sexual behavior in the 1970's–part II: premarital sex." Playboy (November): 74-75.

HURT, M. (1975) "Child abuse and neglect: a report on the status of the research." U.S. Department of Health, Education, and Welfare, Office of Human Development/ Office of Child Development.

JOHNSON, B. and H. MORSE (1968) "Injured children and their parents." Children 15: 147-152.

JUROW, G. (1971) "New data on the effect of a 'death qualified' jury on guilt determination process." Harvard Law Review 85: 567-611.

JUSTICE, B. and R. JUSTICE (1976) The Abusing Family. New York: Human Sciences Press.

KAGAN, J. (1958) "Socialization of aggression and the perception of parents in fantasy." Child Development 29: 311-320.

––– B. HOSKEN, and S. WATSON (1961) "Child's symbolic conceptualization of parents." Child Development 32 (March-December): 625-636.

KAPLAN, H. (1972) "Toward a general theory of psychosocial deviance: the case of aggressive behavior." Social Science and Medicine 6 (5): 593-617.

KATZ, D. and R. KAHN (1966) The Social Psychology of Organizations. New York: John Wiley.

KAUFMAN, W. (1957) "Status, authoritarianism, and anti-semitism." American Journal of Sociology 62: 379-382.

KEMPE, C. (1971) "Pediatric implications of the battered baby syndrome." Archives of Disease in Children 46: 28-37.

––– et al. (1962) "The battered-child syndrome." Journal of the American Medical Association 181 (July 7): 17-24.

KERLINGER, F. (1973) Foundations of Behavioral Research. 2nd ed. New York: Holt, Rinehart, & Winston.

KINSEY, A., B. WARDELL, and C. MARTIN (1948) Sexual Behavior in the Human Male. Philadelphia: W.B. Saunders.

KITSUSE, J. (1964) "Societal reaction to deviant behavior: problems of theory and method," pp. 87-102 in H. Becker (ed.) Perspectives on Deviance–The Other Side. New York: Free Press.

LAING, R. (1971) The Politics of the Family. New York: Vintage.

LAKIN, M. (1957) "Assessment of significant role attitudes in primiparous mothers by means of a modification of the TAT." Psychosomatic Medicine 19: 50-60.

LANDIS, J. (1957) "Values and limitations of family research using student subjects." Marriage and Family Living 19 (February): 100-105.

LAROSSA, R. (1976) "Couples expecting their first child: use of in-depth interviews." Presented to the Population Association of America in Montreal, Canada.

––– (1977) Conflict and Power in Marriage: Expecting the First Child. Beverly Hills: Sage.

LARSEN, O. [ed.] (1968) Violence and the Mass Media. New York: Harper & Row.

LASLETT, B. (1973) "The family as a public and private institution: a historical perspective." Journal of Marriage and the Family 35 (August): 480-492.

––– and R. RAPOPORT (1975) "Collaborative interviewing and interactive research." Journal of Marriage and the Family 37 (November): 968-977.

LeMASTERS, E. (1957) "Parenthood as crisis." Marriage and Family Living 19 (November): 352-355.

LEMERT, E. (1951) Social Pathology. New York: McGraw-Hill.

LENA, H. and S. WARKOV (1974) "Occupational perceptions of child abuse: common and divergent conceptions of a social problem." Presented at the forty-fourth Annual Meetings of the Eastern Sociological Society in Philadelphia.

LEON, C. (1969) "Unusual patterns of crime during 'la Violencia' in Columbia." American Journal of Psychiatry 125 (11): 1564-1575.

LEVINE, R. (1959) "Gussi sex offenses: a study in social control." American Anthropologist 61: 965-990.

LEVINGER, G. (1966) "Sources of marital dissatisfaction among applicants for divorce." American Journal of Orthopsychiatry 26 (October): 803-897. Pp. 126-132 as reprinted in P. Glasser and L. Glasser [eds.] Families in Crisis. New York: Harper & Row.

LIGHT, R. (1974) "Abused and neglected children in America: a study of alternative policies." Harvard Educational Review 43 (November): 556-598.

LOVENS, H. and J. RAKO (1975) "A community approach to the prevention of child abuse." Child Welfare 54 (February): 83-87.

LYMAN, S. and M. SCOTT (1970) A Sociology of the Absurd. New York: Appleton-Century-Crofts.

MAC CARTHY, M. (1963) The Group. New York: Harcourt Brace Jovanovich.

MC CLELLAND, D. (1955) "Notes for a revised theory of motivation," pp. 226-234 in D. McClelland (ed.) Studies in Motivation. New York: Appleton-Century-Crofts.

MARTIN, D. (1976) Battered Wives. San Francisco: Glide.

MAURER, A. (1976) "Physical punishment of children." Presented at the California State Psychological Convention in Anaheim.

MEDIA, A. and K. THOMPSON (1974) Against Rape. New York: Farrar, Straus, and Giroux.

MERTON, R. (1938) "Social structure and anomie." American Sociological Review 3 (October): 672-682.

MEYER, M. and R. TOLMAN (1955) "Correspondence between attitudes and images of parent figures in TAT stories and therapeutic interviews." Journal of Consulting Psychology 19: 79-82.

MILLER, N. (1941) "The frustration-aggression hypothesis." Psychological Review 48: 337-342.

MILLS, C.W. (1940) "Situated actions and vocabularies of motive." American Sociological Review 5 (October): 904-913.

Mindout (1974) What About Battered Wives? London: MIND National Association for Mental Health.

MITCHELL, M. (1936) Gone With the Wind. New York: Macmillan.

MORGAN, P. and E. GAIER (1956) "The direction of aggression in the mother-child situation." Child Development 27: 447-457.

MORRIS, M., R. GOULD, and P. MATTHEWS (1964) "Toward prevention of child abuse." Children 2 (March-April): 55-60.

NAGI, R. (1975) "Child abuse and neglect programs: a national overview." Children Today 4 (May-June): 13-17.

New York Radical Feminists (1974) Rape: The First Sourcebook for Women. New York: New American Library.

NEWBERGER, E. and R. BOURNE (1978) "The medicalization and legalization of child abuse." American Journal of Orthopsychiatry 48 (October): 593-607.

——— et al. (1977) "Pediatric social illness: toward an etiologic classification." Pediatrics 60: 178-185.

——— G. HAAS, and R. MULFORD (1973) "Child abuse in Massachusetts: incidence, current mechanism for intervention, and recommendations for effective control."

Massachusetts Physician 32: (January): 31-38.

——— and J. HYDE (1975) "Child abuse: principles and implications of current pediatric practice." Pediatric Clinics of North America 22 (August): 695-715.

——— R. REED, J. DANIEL, J. HYDE, and M. KOTELCHUCK (1975) "Toward an etiological classification of pediatric social illness: a descriptive epidemiology of child abuse and neglect, failure to thrive accidents, and poisonings in children under four years of age." Presented at the biennial meetings of the Society for Research on Child Development in Denver.

Newsweek (1973) "Britain: battered wives." July 9: 39.

NYE, F. and A. BAYER (1963) "Some recent trends in family research." Social Forces 41: 290-301.

O'BRIEN, J. (1971) "Violence in divorce prone families." Journal of Marriage and the Family 33 (November): 692-698.

ORNE, M. (1962) "On the social psychology of the psychological experiment: with particular reference to demand characteristics and their importance." American Psychologist 17: 776-783.

OWENS, D. and M. STRAUS (1975) "Childhood violence and adult approval of violence." Aggressive Behavior 1 (2): 193-211.

PALMER, S. (1972) The Violent Society. New Haven: College and University Press.

——— (1962) The Psychology of Murder. New York: Thomas Y. Crowell Co.

PARNAS, R. (1967) "The police response to domestic disturbance." Wisconsin Law Review 914 (Fall): 914-960.

PAULSON, M. and P. BLAKE (1969) "The physically abused child: a focus on prevention." Child Welfare 48 (February): 86-95.

Pediatric News (1975) "One child dies daily from abuse: parent probably was abuser." Volume 9 (April): 3.

PELTON, L. (1978) "Child abuse and neglect: the myth of classlessness." American Journal of Orthopsychiatry 48 (October): 608-617.

PETERS, J. (1975) "The Philadelphia rape victim study," pp. 181-199 in I. Drapkin and E. Viano (eds.) Victimology: A New Focus Vol. 3. Lexington, MA: Lexington Books.

PFOHL, S. (1977) "The 'discovery' of child abuse." Social Problems 24 (3): 310-323.

PHILLIPS, D. (1971) Knowledge From What? Theories and Methods in Social Research. Chicago: Rand McNally.

PLECK, E, J. PLECK, M. GROSSMAN, and P. BART (1977) "The battered data syndrome: a comment on Steinmetz's article." Victimology 2 (3/4): 680-683.

POLAKOW, R. and D. PEABODY (1975) "Behavioral treatment of child abuse." International Journal of Offender Therapy and Comparative Criminology 19: 100ff.

POLANSKY, M., R. BORGMAN, and C. DESAIX (1972) Roots of Futility. San Francisco: Jossey-Bass.

POLSKY, N. (1969) Hustlers, Beats and Others. Garden City, NY: Anchor.

POMEROY, W. (1966) "Human sexual behavior," pp. 22-32 in N. Farberow (ed.) Taboo Topics. New York: Atherton Press.

PRESCOTT, J. and C. MC KAY (1973) "Child abuse and child care: some cross cultural and anthropological perspectives." Presented at the National Conference on Child Abuse in Washington, DC (June).

PRESCOTT, S. and C. LETKO (1977) "Battered women: a social psychological perspective," pp. 72-96 in M. Roy (ed.) Battered Women: A Psychosociological Study of Domestic Violence. New York: Van Nostrand Reinhold.

PUZO, M. (1969) The Godfather. New York: Putnam.

RADBILL, S. (1974) "A history of child abuse and infanticide," pp. 3-24 in R. Helfer and C. Kempe (eds.) The Battered Child. 2nd ed Chicago: University of Chicago Press.

RADKE, M. (1946) "The relation of parental authority to children's behavior and attitudes." University of Minnesota Child Welfare Monographs, 22.

RANULF, S. (1964) Moral Indignation and Middle Class Psychology—A Sociological Study. New York: Schocken.

REINER, B. and I. KAUFMAN (1959) Character Disorders in Parents of Delinquents. New York: Family Service Association of America.

REISS, I. (1960) Premarital Sexual Standards in America. New York: Free Press.

RESNICK, P. (1969) "Child murder by parents: a psychiatric review of filicide." American Journal of Psychiatry 126 (3): 325-334.

RIEKEN, H. et al. (1954) "Narrowing the gap between field studies and laboratory experiment in social psychology: a statement of the summer seminar." Social Science Research Council Items 8 (December): 37-42.

ROBERTS, A. and R. JESSOR (1958) "Authoritarianism, punitiveness, and perceived social status." Journal of Abnormal and Social Psychology 56: 311-314.

——— and M. ROKEACH (1956) "Anomie, authoritarianism and prejudice: a replication." American Journal of Sociology 61: 355-358.

ROBINSON, J., R. ATHANASIOU, and K. HEAD (1969) Measures of Occupational Attitudes and Occupational Characteristics. Ann Arbor, MI: Survey Research Center.

ROKEACH, M. and D. MC CLELLAND (1969-1970) "Dogmatism and the death penalty: a reinterpretation of the Duquesne poll data." Duquesne Law Review 8: 125-129.

——— and N. VIDMAR (1973) "Testimony concerning possible jury bias in a Black Panther trial." Journal of Applied Social Psychology 3 (1): 19-29.

ROSSI, A. (1968) "Transition to parenthood." Journal of Marriage and the Family 30 (February): 26-39.

ROTH, J. (1966) "Hired hand research." American Sociologist 1 (August): 190-196.

RUSSELL, D. (1975) The Politics of Rape: The Victim's Perspective. New York: Stein and Day.

SANDERS, R. (1972) "Resistance to dealing with parents of battered children." Pediatrics 50 (December): 853-857.

SCANZONI, J. (1972) Sexual Bargaining. Englewood Cliffs, NJ: Prentice-Hall.

SCHAFER, S. (1968) The Victim and His Criminal: A Study in Functional Responsibility. New York: Random House.

SCHEFF, T. (1966) "Negotiating reality: notes on power in the assessment of responsibility." Social Problems 16 (Summer): 3-17.

SCHULTZ, D. (1969) Coming Up Black: Patterns of Ghetto Socialization. Englewood Cliffs, NJ: Prentice-Hall.

SCHWARTZ, R. and J. SKOLNICK (1964) "Two studies of legal stigma," pp. 103-117 in H. Becker (ed.) Perspectives on Deviance—The Other Side. New York: Free Press.

SCOTT, M. and S. LYMAN (1968) "Accounts." American Sociological Review 33 (1): 46-62.

SEITES, J. (1975) "Marital rape: dispelling the myth." (unpublished)

SELLTIZ, C. et al. (1959) Research Methods in Social Relations. New York: Holt, Rinehart & Winston.

SHAH, S. (1970a) "Recent developments in human genetics and their implication for problems of social deviance." Paper presented at the American Association for the Advancement of Science in Chicago (December).

——— (1970b) "Report on the XYY chromosomal abnormality." National Institutes of Mental Health Conference Report. Washington, D.C.: Government Printing Office.

SHNEIDMAN, E. (1966) "Suicide," pp. 33-43 in N. Farberow (ed.) Taboo Topics. New York: Atherton Press.

SHORTER, E. (1975) The Making of the Modern Family. New York: Basic Books.

SILVERMAN, F. (1953) "The roentgen manifestations of unrecognized skeletal trauma in infants." American Journal of Roentgenology, Radium Therapy, and Nuclear Medicine 69: 413-427.

SILVERMAN, S. (1976) "Rape in marriage: is it legal?" Do It Now (June): 10.

SIMMEL, G. (1950) The Sociology of Georg Simmel (K. Wolf ed.). New York: Free Press.

SIMMONS, J. (1965) "Public stereotypes of deviants." Social Problems 3 (Fall): 223-232.

SINGER, J. [ed.] (1971) The Control of Aggression and Violence. New York: Academic Press.

SKOLNICK, A. and J. SKOLNICK [eds.] (1977) The Family in Transition, 2nd edition. Boston: Little, Brown.

SMITH, H. and E. ROSEN (1958) "Some psychological correlates of world mindedness and authoritarianism." Journal of Personality 26: 170-183.

SNELL, J., R. ROSENWALD, and A. ROBEY (1964) "The wifebeater's wife: a study of family interaction." Archives of General Psychiatry 11 (August): 107-113.

SNORTUM, J. and V. ASHEAR (1972) "Prejudice, punitiveness, and personality." Journal of Personality Assessment 36: 291-296.

SOKOL, R. (1976) "Some factors associated with child abuse potential." Presented at the annual meetings of the American Sociological Association in New York.

SPINETTA, J. and D. RIGLER (1972) "The child abusing parent: a psychological review." Psychological Bulletin 77 (April): 296-304.

SROLE, L., T. LANGNER, S. MICHAEL, M. OPLER and T. RENNIE (1962) Mental Health in the Metropolis. New York: McGraw-Hill.

STARK, R. and J. MC EVOY (1970) "Middle class violence." Psychology Today 4 (November): 52-65.

STARR, J. and N. CUTLER (1972) "Sex role and attitudes toward institutional violence among college youth: the impact of sex-role identification, parental socialization and socio-cultural milieu. Presented at the meetings of the American Sociological Association.

STEELE, B. and C. POLLOCK (1968) "A psychiatric study of parents who abuse infants and small children," pp. 103-147 in R. Helfer and C. Kempe (eds.) The Battered Child. Chicago: University of Chicago Press.

——— (1974) "A psychiatric study of parents who abuse infants and small children," pp. 89-134 in R. Helfer and C. Kempe (eds.) The Battered Child. 2nd ed. Chicago: University of Chicago Press.

STEINMETZ, S. (1971) "Occupation and physical punishment: a response to Straus." Journal of Marriage and the Family 33 (November): 664-666.

——— (1974) "Occupational environment in relation to physical punishment and dogmatism," pp. 166-172 in S. Steinmetz and M. Straus (eds.) Violence in the Family. New York: Harper & Row.

——— (1975) "Intra-familial patterns of conflict resolution: husband/wife; parent/child; sibling/sibling." Ph.D. dissertation. Cleveland: Case Western Reserve University.

——— (1977) "The battered husband syndrome." Victimology 2 (3/4): 499-509.

——— and M. STRAUS (1971) "Some myths about violence in the family." Presented at the meetings of the American Sociological Association.

——— and M. STRAUS (1973a) "Five myths about violence in the family." (mimeograph).

――― and M. STRAUS (1973b) "The family as cradle of violence." Society 10 (September/October): 50-56.

――― and M. STRAUS (1974) Violence in the Family. New York: Harper & Row.

STRAUS, M. (1969) "Phenomenal identity and conceptual equivalence of measurement in cross-national research." Journal of Marriage and the Family 31 (May): 233-239.

――― (1971) "Some social antecedents of physical punishment: a linkage theory interpretation." Journal of Marriage and the Family 33 (November): 658-663.

――― (1973) "A general systems theory approach to a theory of violence between family members." Social Science Information 12 (June): 105-125.

――― (1974a) "Cultural and social organization influences on violence between family members," pp. 53-69 in R. Prince and D. Barrier (eds.) Configurations: Biological and Cultural Factors in Sexuality and Family Life. Lexington, MA: Heath.

――― (1974b) "Leveling, civility, and violence in the family." Journal of Marriage and the Family 36 (February): 13-30.

――― (1976) "Sexual inequality, cultural norms, and wife beating." Victimology 1: 54-76.

――― (1977a) "A sociological perspective on the prevention and treatment of wife-beating," pp. 194-238 in Maria Roy (ed.) Battered Women: A Psychosociological Study of Domestic Violence. New York: Van Nostrand Reinhold.

――― (1977b) "Societal morphogenesis and intrafamily violence in cross-cultural perspective." Annals of the New York Academy of Science. 285: 717-730.

――― (1979a) "A sociological perspective on the causes of family violence." Presented at the annual meetings of the American Association for the Advancement of Science, Houston.

――― (1979b) "Family patterns and child abuse in a nationally representative American sample." International Journal of Child Abuse and Neglect. (in press)

――― (1979c) "Measuring intrafamily conflict and violence: the conflict tactics (CT) scales." Journal of Marriage and the Family 41. (February): 75-88.

――― and S. CYTRYNBAUM (1961) A Scoring Manual for Intra-familial Power and Affective Support. Minneapolis: Minnesota Family Study Center.

――― R. GELLES, and S. STEINMETZ (1973) "Theories, methods, and controversies in the study of violence between family members." Presented at meetings of the American Sociological Association.

――― (1976) "Violence in the family: an assessment of knowledge and research needs." Presented to the American Association for the Advancement of Science in Boston.

――― (1979) Behind Closed Doors: Violence in the American Family. New York: Doubleday/Anchor. (in press)

――― and G. HOTALING (1979) The Social Causes of Husband-Wife Violence. Minneapolis, MN: University of Minnesota Press. (in press)

――― and I. TALLMAN (1971) "SIMFAM: a technique for observational measurement and experimental study of families," pp. 378-438 in J. Aldous et al. (eds.) Family Problem Solving. Hinsdale, Il: Dryden.

SUDNOW, D. (1964) "Normal crimes: sociological features of the penal code in a public defender office." Social Problems 12 (3): 255-276.

SZASZ, T. (1960) "The myth of mental illness." American Psychologist 15 (February): 113-118.

――― (1961) The Myth of Mental Illness: Foundations of a Theory of Personal Conduct. New York: Delta.

――― (1970) The Manufacture of Madness. New York: Harper & Row.

TANAY, E. (1969) Psychiatric study of homicide. American Journal of Psychiatry 125 (a): 1252-1258.

TEN BROECK, E. (1974) "The extended family center: 'a home away from home' for abused children and their parents." Children Today 3 (April): 2-6.

THOMAS, C. Unpublished study.

——— and S. FOSTER (1975) "A sociological perspective on public support for capital punishment." American Journal of Orthopsychiatry 45 (July): 641-657.

THOMPSON, J. (1966) Organizations in Action. New York: McGraw-Hill.

TRUNINGER, E. (1971) "Marital violence: the legal solutions." Hastings Law Review 23 (November): 259-276.

U.S. Bureau of the Census (1975) "Estimates of the population of the United States by age, sex, and race: 1970-1975. Current Population Reports, Series P-25, 614. Washington, DC: U.S. Government Printing Office.

U.S. Department of Health, Education and Welfare (1969) Bibliography on the Battered Child. Social and Rehabilitation Service, July.

United States Senate (1973) Hearing Before the Subcommittee on Children and Youth of the Committee on Labor and Public Welfare. United States Senate, 93rd Congress, First Session on S.1191 Child Abuse Prevention Act. Washington, D.C.: U.S. Government Printing Office.

VIANO, E. (1974) "Attitudes toward child abuse among American professionals." Presented at the First Meetings of the International Society for Research on Aggression, Toronto, Canada.

VIDMAR, N. and P. ELLSWORTH (1974) "Public opinion and the death penalty." Stanford Law Review 26 (6): 1245-1270.

WARNER, S. (1965) "Randomized response: a survey technique for eliminating evasive answer bias." American Statistical Association 60: 63-69.

WASSERMAN, S. (1967) "The abused parent of the abused child." Children 14 (September-October): 175-179.

WEATHERLY, D. (1963) "Maternal response to childhood aggression and subsequent anti-Semitism." Journal of Abnormal and Social Psychology 66: 183-185.

WEBB, E. et al. (1966) Unobtrusive Measures. Chicago: Rand McNally.

Webster's New Collegiate Dictionary (1975) Springfield, MA: Merriam.

WHITING, B. (1975) Personal communication.

WHYTE, W. (1955) Street Corner Society. Chicago: University of Chicago Press.

WOLFGANG, M. (1957) Victim-precipitated criminal homicide. Journal of Criminal Law, Criminology and Police Science 48 (June): 1-11.

——— and F. FERRACUTI (1967) The Subculture of Violence. London: Tavistock Publications.

WOLKENSTEIN, A. (1975) "Hospital acts on child abuse." Journal of the American Hospital Association 49 (March): 103-106.

WOOLLEY, P. and W. EVANS (1955) "Significance of skeletal lesions resembling those of traumatic origin." Journal of the American Medical Association 158: 539-543.

YOUNG, L. (1964) Wednesday's Child: A Study of Child Neglect and Abuse. New York: McGraw-Hill.

ZALBA, S. (1971) "Battered children." Transaction 8 (July-August): 58-61.

ZIGLER, E. (1976) "Controlling child abuse in America: an effort doomed to failure." Presented at the First National Conference on Child Abuse and Neglect in Atlanta (January).

ABOUT THE AUTHOR

RICHARD J. GELLES is Associate Professor and Chair of the Department of Sociology and Anthropology at the University of Rhode Island. He has published extensively on the topics of child abuse, wife abuse, and family violence. He is the author of THE VIOLENT HOME (Sage Publications, 1974) and is the coauthor of BEHIND CLOSED DOORS: VIOLENCE IN THE AMERICAN FAMILY (Anchor/Doubleday, 1979).

NOTES

NOTES